BEAUTY AND THE BIBLE

Society of Biblical Literature

Series

Gerald O. West, General Editor

Editorial Board:
Pablo Andiñach
Fiona Black
Denise K. Buell
Gay L. Byron
Jione Havea
Jennifer L. Koosed
Jeremy Punt
Yak-Hwee Tan

Number 73
Board Editor: Jennifer L. Koosed

BEAUTY AND THE BIBLE

TOWARD A HERMENEUTICS OF BIBLICAL AESTHETICS

Edited by

Richard J. Bautch and Jean-François Racine

Society of Biblical Literature
Atlanta

Library of Congress Cataloging-in-Publication Data

Beauty and the Bible / edited by Richard J. Bautch and Jean-François Racine.
     p. cm. — (Society of Biblical Literature. Semeia studies ; number 73)
    Includes bibliographical references and index.
    ISBN 978-1-58983-907-6 (paper binding : alk. paper) — ISBN 978-1-58983-908-3 (electronic format) — ISBN 978-1-58983-909-0 (hardcover binding : alk. paper)
    1. Aesthetics in the Bible. 2. Bible—Criticism, interpretation, etc. I. Bautch, Richard J. II. Racine, Jean-François.
    BS680.A33B43 2013
    220.6—dc23   2013030910

Printed on acid-free, recycled paper conforming to
ANSI/NISO Z39.48-1992 (R1997) and ISO 9706:1994
standards for paper permanence.

For Gina Hens-Piazza and David Penchansky

Contents

ABBREVIATIONS

AA	Ann Arbor Paperbacks
AB	Anchor Bible
AOTC	Abingdon Old Testament Commentaries
BA	*Biblical Archaeologist*
BAR	*Biblical Archaeology Review*
Bib	*Biblica*
BZAW	Beihefte zur Zeitschrift für die alttestamentliche Wissenschaft
CBA	Catholic Biblical Association
CBQ	*Catholic Biblical Quarterly*
EJL	Early Judaism and Its Literature
EKKNT	Evangelisch-katholischer Kommentar zum Neuen Testament
ExAud	*Ex auditu*
FOTL	Forms of the Old Testament Literature
JETS	*Journal of the Evangelical Theological Society*
JSJ	*Journal for the Study of Judaism in the Persian, Hellenistic, and Roman Periods*
JSNTSup	Journal for the Study of the New Testament: Supplement Series
JSOT	*Journal for the Study of the Old Testament*
LCL	Loeb Classical Library
LHBOTS	Library of Hebrew Bible/Old Testament Studies
LXX	Septuagint
NICNT	New International Commentary on the New Testament
NJB	New Jerusalem Bible
NRSV	New Revised Standard Version
NTS	*New Testament Studies*
OTL	Old Testament Library
PEQ	*Palestine Exploration Quarterly*

PhB	Philosophischen Bibliothek
RB	*Revue biblique*
RelArts	Religion and the Arts
SBLDS	Society of Biblical Literature Dissertation Series
SP	Sacra Pagina
UTB	Uni-Taschenbücher
ZRGG	Zeitschrift für Religions- und Geistesgeschichte

INTRODUCTION

There are distinct challenges involved in articulating a hermeneutics of biblical aesthetics in the twenty-first century. *Beauty and the Bible: Toward a Hermeneutics of Biblical Aesthetics* is conceived as a response to three such challenges. First, the turn to subjectivity in the philosophy of the Enlightenment must be addressed in terms of its impact on the notion of beauty, biblical and otherwise. Immanuel Kant's *Critique of Judgment*, for example, is crucial background for understanding modern aesthetic concepts like sublimity and for engaging approaches to the text, such as reader response, that are informed by critical theory. Critical theory in general has decentered aesthetics and highlighted the subject's role in the determination of beauty. These developments are traced back to Kant and his impact on modern thought.

A second challenge relates to context, the aggregate of historical factors that prevent us from ever again conceiving of "art for art's sake." The composition of each biblical book, along with the history of its reception, is fraught with the minutiae of politics, economics, gender, and global interdependencies. These factors can create a context that is morally ambiguous with evidence of inequity, exploitation, and even atrocity. How does beauty function in such circumstances? Although there are many possibilities, lest beauty become the veneer that conceals all manner of inconvenient truths, it should be viewed through the lenses of new historicism, postcolonialism, and similar hermeneutics of suspicion. Such approaches attend to ideologies that may mark the biblical texts and their interpretation.

The pendulum's swing signals a third challenge, to approach the biblical text postcritically. Increasingly, there are readers of the Bible with eyes wide open but looking beyond the learning of philosophers or critical theorists. Such reading may sidestep the epistemological turn made by Kant in order to recover a concept of beauty said to be more relevant to the ancient mind. A postcritical reading seeks, among other things, an understanding of the nature of beauty that is grounded in semantics and the language of the text. With this type of reading, beauty's power of attraction provides the grounds for aesthetic theology.

In short, a volume on contemporary biblical aesthetics with the requisite breadth and depth will delve into modern philosophy, contextual criticism, and the postcritical return to beauty's intrinsic qualities. While these three perspectives are quite different and not to be harmonized, exploring them concurrently in this volume serves each in turn and produces a study with intriguing methodological tensions. These are the type of tensions that can be profitably explored for the insights they may yield. *Beauty and the Bible: Toward a Hermeneutics of Biblical Aesthetics* is designed to serve a wide readership, with each reader resonating with one or perhaps two of the challenges indicated above. Additionally, readers may have an unanticipated and uncanny engagement with that "other" approach to biblical beauty that they might otherwise discount. These essays offer new perspectives on beauty in the Bible and a range of hermeneutical tools to advance the study of aesthetics.

In its complement of essays on beauty in the Bible, this book introduces readers to modern philosophy, to contextual criticism, and to the postcritical return to beauty. Modern philosophy informs "The Potential of the Category of Sublime for Reading the Episodes of the Stilling of the Storm (Luke 8:22–25) and of the Transfiguration (Luke 9:28–36)," by Jean-François Racine. After reviewing the association of the sublime and terror in Western thought, this essay reads the stories of the calming of the storm and the transfiguration in Luke as prompting an experience of the sublime. "The Sublime Art of Prophetic Seeing and the Word in the Book of Jeremiah," by Mark Brummitt, continues in this vein. Brummitt considers the proliferation of meanings in Jeremiah's words and body as an instance of the sublime. He finds resonance of this phenomenon in the British painter Francis Bacon (1908–1992), whose work serves as a lens to look at Jeremiah. The role of subjectivity in critical theory is at the center of "Perceiving Beauty in Mark 5:21–43," by Antonio Portalatín. This essay turns to Wolfgang Iser's theory of reading as an aesthetic response to highlight the pleasurable aspects of reading the story of the hemorrhaging woman and the resurrection of Jairus's daughter in the fifth chapter of Mark.

David Penchansky's essay, "Beauty, Power, and Attraction: Aesthetics and the Hebrew Bible," serves as a primer on contextual criticism. Penchansky examines the vocabulary of beauty in the Hebrew Bible and uses the test cases of Rachel and David to investigate further the relationship between beauty and power. Embedded in Penchansky's analysis is the presupposition that texts, particularly old, sacred texts that have passed through many hands and many communities, are sites of conflict. Rather than looking for a particular objective meaning, a reading should uncover the conflicts, contradictions, and places of dissonance within a text. Paired with Penchansky's essay is an empirical study, "Yachin and Boaz in Jerusalem and Rome" by Richard Bautch. This essay deals with the columns Yachin and Boaz in the Solomonic Temple, curiously described in 1 Kings and 2 Chronicles. Bautch first looks at how these columns were rearticulated in Christian architecture and argues that what made the Solomonic columns especially attractive to artists of the Renaissance was that the two pillars reflected aesthetic and political dimensions of the society that created them. A broader conclusion is that history provides multiple examples of a leader seeking political gain by associating himself with a stunning architectural feature from the temple of Solomon.

Jo-Ann Brant's postcritical reading of beauty in the Gospel of John identifies an aesthetic dimension to Johannine theology and Christology. Such an aesthetic, she indicates, is essential to the Johannine notion of glory and revelation. Moreover, as an aesthetic object, the Gospel of John is not simply an account of what happened but a work of art that imparts a sense of divine beauty by means of the beauty of the prose. That is, the biblical writer seems to understand that God's glory is perceivable to the physical senses and not simply the mind's eye. Brant's essay is informed by the thought of Simone Weil and Han Urs von Balthasar.

The final essay, by Peter Spitaler, serves as an epilogue to the volume. Responding to all the essays, Spitaler highlights common themes and motifs in the various biblical narratives and underscores hermeneutical insights that are shared by the contributors. Without imposing unity, Spitaler synthesizes the studies in this collection by focusing on three aspects: the historical, social, and cultural boundedness of beauty constructs; the subjective dimension in the perception of beauty; and the relationships between the beautiful and the sublime. Spitaler concludes with suggestions for further research on beauty, Bible, method, and hermeneutics. The collection of essays as a whole underscores the significance of aesthetics and related considerations for the ancient writers of sacred texts and for individuals and communities who read them today with modern and postmodern sensibilities.

These explorations into the aesthetic qualities of seven discrete biblical texts signal a fresh, interdisciplinary understanding of scripture. More than ever, beauty is in the eyes of the beholder to suggest great diversity in the field of aesthetics and new challenges for readers of the Bible. Moreover, *Beauty and the Bible: Toward a Hermeneutics of Biblical Aesthetics* catalogs the plurality of methods currently in use to elaborate and comment on beauty in the biblical text. The diversity reflected on these pages parallels that of the volume's contributors in the aggregate. That is, while two of the authors are from the continental United States, five come from other cultural contexts that include the Caribbean, continental Europe, French-speaking Canada, and Great Britain. Amid this diversity, there has been an abiding center: many of these essays were conceived within a working group on hermeneutics that meets as part of the international meeting of the Catholic Biblical Association of America. In sessions from 2008 to 2010, the group considered and critiqued one another's studies on biblical aesthetics, and the project developed into *Beauty and the Bible: Toward a Hermeneutics of Biblical Aesthetics.*

The editors acknowledge and express gratitude to the Catholic Biblical Association of America for its support of this project. We also thank the editors at Semeia Studies, Jennifer Koosed and Gerald West, along with the editorial staff at the Society of Biblical Literature, especially Kathie Klein, Bob Buller, and Leigh Andersen. We thank as well our research assistant, Peter Claver Ajer, for his work on the indices. Finally, we dedicate this volume to Gina Hens-Piazza and David Penchansky. For many years Gina and David led the study of hermeneutics within the Catholic Biblical Association of America by convening the group that meets annually at the international meeting. In this role, they were among the first to conceive and articulate a synthesis between biblical studies and critical theory. Their leadership advanced the study of biblical hermeneutics at a critical time in its development, and under their influence an entire cohort of scholars came to approach the biblical text with methodological savvy and a concomitant desire to be of service, to the world and to communities of faith. In the field of hermeneutics, the legacy of Gina and David is a thing of beauty.

The Potential of the Category of Sublime for Reading the Episodes of the Stilling of the Storm (Luke 8:22–25) and of the Transfiguration (Luke 9:28–36)

Jean-François Racine

1. Introduction

The last twenty years or so have seen the rise of sports qualified as "extreme sports." One may think about bungee jumping, ice climbing, and even downhill ice skating in the steep streets of Québec City. Some of these sports allow one to confront difficult natural conditions or even to experience a situation that normally would result in death, as in the case of bungee jumping. In other words, some "extreme sports" allow one to savor the "big chill." As one goes through the various episodes of a Gospel such as Luke, one may perceive that the disciples have several opportunities to experience that "big chill" as they follow Jesus.

I suggest that a reader or a listener absorbed in the unfolding of the story may also experience some stronger emotions while going through episodes of a Gospel such as the stilling of the storm and the transfiguration than while reading, let us say, the genealogy of Jesus found in Luke 3:23–38 or the parable of the persistent widow in Luke 18:1–6. I also suggest that if the phrase "big chill" may be useful to convey the emotions likely or explicitly felt by the characters of these episodes, the notion of sublime is useful to describe what the committed reader/listener may experience.

The approach presented here to the episodes of the stilling of the storm and of the transfiguration in Luke 8:22–25 and 9:28–36 is therefore definitely reader oriented: I am interested in the peculiarity of a reader's feelings before certain passages of the Third Gospel. As a corollary, I am also interested in the specific qualities of these passages that prompt these feelings. At the present moment, I envision the notion of sublime heuristically rather than hermeneutically. It may serve to put words on an experience that comes from reading some biblical passages and to understand what prompts this type of experience.

The first part of this paper briefly explores the notion of the sublime. For that purpose, it considers the work of Longinus, which constitutes the first known attempt in the West to tackle that issue. Thereafter, the discussion jumps over more than fifteen centuries to focus on the reception of Longinus in seventeenth-century France and especially in eighteenth-century Great Britain, before dealing with the Kantian notion of sublime. Once that groundwork is done, the paper attempts a reading of the stories of the stilling of the storm and of the transfiguration in Luke using insights gathered from Longinus, various seventeenth- and eighteenth-century French and British thinkers, and Immanuel Kant. Finally, it reflects on the assets and limitations of a reading strategy based on the sublime and suggests possible directions for further research.

2. *On the Sublime*, by Longinus

The treatise Περὶ ὕψους (*On the Sublime*) has been attributed to Dionysos Longinus or Cassius Longinus, depending on the manuscripts. It was likely written during the first century C.E. by a Hellenized Jew with an interest in the concept of the sublime; one of the first examples it cites of the sublime is a verse from the creation story found in Genesis. It is worthy of attention not only as a historical artifact but also because, as Samuel Monk (1960, 15) explains, "Longinus was to become the patron saint of much that is unclassical and unneoclassical, and eventually of much that is romantic, in eighteenth-century England."

The goal of the treatise is to teach useful rhetorical devices to persuade an audience. Unlike works written, for instance, by Aristotle or Hermagoras, the treatise highlights the sublime type, which does not have specific forms, especially in comparison with common types such as judicial, epideictic, and deliberative. Longinus first points to the effect of the sublime on an audience: "A well-timed flash of sublimity shatters everything like a bolt of lightning and reveals the full power of the speaker at a single stroke" (*Subl.* 1). Additionally, the effect of the sublime "is not to persuade the audience but rather to transport them out of themselves. Invariably what inspires wonder, with its power of amazing us, always prevails over what is merely convincing and pleasing." Thereafter, Longinus explains faults that prevent authors from exhibiting sublimity: outbursts of emotion that are private to the speaker (tumidity), puerility, and frigidity (*Subl.* 3–4).

The pedagogical value of the treatise is nevertheless problematic, first, because it never indicates how to recognize the sublime except by the impression it makes on the listener. Second, it only provides the so-called sources of the sublime—grand conceptions; inspiration of vehement emotions; proper construction of figures of thought and figures of speech; nobility of language; and dignified and elevated word arrangement (*Subl.* 8)—without saying exactly what these are or how to bring them together. From the various comments scattered around the treatise, one realizes that the sublime may sometimes have little to do with emotions as Longinus provides examples of simple phrases that he considers as sublime. At times, it may simply correspond to episodical sparks of genius that may not have much to do with correct style (*Subl.* 33). Still, these sparks of genius must refer to something grand, as Longinus assumes that the human being is instinctively drawn by the grand that is first encountered in nature.

> Look at life from all sides and see how in all things the extraordinary, the great, the beautiful stand supreme, and you will soon realize what we were born for. So it is by some natural instinct that we admire, not the small streams, clear and useful as they are, but the Nile, the Danube, the Rhine, and above all the Ocean. The little fire we kindle for ourselves keeps clear and steady, yet we do not therefore regard it with more amazement than the fires of Heaven, which are often darkened, or think it more wonderful than the craters of Etna in eruption, hurling up rocks and whole hills from their depths and sometimes shooting forth rivers of that earthborn, spontaneous fire. But on all such matters I would only say this, that what is useful or necessary is easily obtained by man; it is always the unusual which wins our wonder. (*Subl.* 33)

Finally, Longinus emphasizes the role of visual imaginations in the sublime. He nevertheless seems to locate the use of visual imagination in the speaker who produces the speech rather than in the audience.

As one perceives, Longinus locates the sublime in the language itself. Accordingly, one may infer that objects and events themselves are not sublime; it is language that makes them so. Yet Longinus is not uninterested in objects, as he names natural phenomena such as the oceans, important rivers, and volcanoes. He is not uninterested either in the emotions of the audience as it is exposed to sublime language. The history of the notion of the sublime in the West indicates that Longinus's treatise set the agenda for the investigation of this concept. Writers from the seventeenth and eighteenth centuries will find in Longinus all the necessary elements to take the notion in very different directions. In addition, if the question of the sublime will become from the eighteenth century forward an aesthetic question, Longinus's rhetorical approach, which locates the sublime in language, has resurfaced in the work of Jacques Derrida, for instance, in *La vérité en peinture* (1978).

3. THE SEVENTEENTH AND EIGHTEENTH CENTURIES

Longinus's treatise and the topic of the sublime vanished in the West until its translation into French by Nicolas Boileau-Despréaux in 1674. Boileau's translation gave Longinus's *On the Sublime* much exposure in Europe, especially in Great Britain. Interestingly enough, Boileau's reading of the treatise makes it support "simplicity of language," which was one of the canons of the neoclassical code. While the French rested content with such an interpretation of *On the Sublime*, thinkers of the British Isles took different directions in interpreting the treatise by turning their attention toward the pathetic and the failure of literary rules to achieve the sublime. The British take on the sublime was also tainted with certain features of British intellectual life of that period, for example, a strong interest in nature and its phenomena.[1] The next part of this section concentrates on the works of four British intellectuals: John Dennis, Joseph Addison, John Baillie, and Edmund Burke.

The literary critic John Dennis (1657–1734) addressed the notion of the sublime as he reflected on the chief ingredient of poetry, which he identified as "passion" (Ashfield and de Bolla 1996, 32). However, there is for Dennis "passion," and there is "passion," as he distinguished ordinary passion from enthusiasm (33).

According to Dennis, enthusiasm proceeds from the thoughts of the subject. Soon Dennis connected enthusiasm to the sublime by means of the "poetic genius": "We may venture to lay down this definition of poetical genius: … poetic genius, is the power of expressing such passion worthily: and the sublime is a great thought, expressed with the enthusiasm that

---

1. It is at that period that some Britons started venturing in the Alps and wrote their accounts of these excursions.

belongs to it" (Ashfield and de Bolla 1996, 34). The connection becomes even stronger at the end of the paragraph as Dennis summarizes his reading of the first seven chapters of Longinus's treatise to state that, if the treatise had described the effects of the sublime, he has identified its causes:

> These are the effects that Longinus tells us, the sublime produces in the minds of men. Now I have endeavoured to show, what is in poetry that works these effects. So that, take the cause and the effects together, and you have the sublime. (Ashfield and de Bolla 1996, 34)

Dennis's second work, *The Grounds of Criticism in Poetry* (1704), carries on the causes or origins of the sublime by identifying six specific enthusiastic passions: admiration, terror, horror, joy, sadness, desire. As passions, they differ from similar emotions encountered in daily life. The poet arrives at them through meditation:

> And here I desire the reader to observe, that ideas in meditation are often very different from what ideas of the same objects are, in the course of common conversation. As for example, the sun mentioned in ordinary conversation, gives the idea of a round flat shining body, of about two foot diameter. But the sun occurring to us in meditation, gives the idea of a vast and glorious body, and at the top of all the visible creation, and the brightest material image of the divinity. (Ashfield and de Bolla 1996, 35–36)

Soon after, these six enthusiastic passions seem to be subsumed under a single one: terror! Dennis associates terror primarily with religious ideas, for "since the more their objects are powerful, and likely to hurt, the greater terror their ideas produce; what can produce a greater terror than the idea of an angry god?" Dennis maintains that Longinus's treatise supports his focus on terror as the source of the passions that can produce the sublime.

> All the examples that Longinus brings of the loftiness of the thought, consist of terrible ideas.... No passion is attended with greater joy than enthusiastic terror, which proceeds from our reflecting that we are out of a danger at the very time that we see it before us. And as terror is one of the violentest of all passions, if it is very great, and the hardest to be resisted, nothing gives more force, no more vehemence to a discourse. (Ashfield and de Bolla 1996, 37–38)

As one perceives from his emphasis on the pathetic, especially terror, Dennis's reading of Longinus deeply differs from Boileau's. His interest in, or rather, fascination with terror persists among several major thinkers through the eighteenth century in Great Britain and will pass to Kant. Still, Dennis locates the sublime in language as did Longinus and even adds, in regard to danger as a trigger of terror, "that it signifies nothing at all to the purpose whether the danger is real or imaginary" (Ashfield and de Bolla 1996, 39).

Joseph Addison (1672–1719), cofounder and regular contributor of the daily publication *The Spectator*, propelled the discussion of the sublime into the public sphere. Dennis had approached the sublime through poetry and a quality that he had named "enthusiasm." Addison approached it under the disguise of "greatness," which he defines as "not only the bulk of any single object, but the largeness of a whole view, considered as one entire piece.... Our imagination loves to be filled with an object, or to grasp at any thing that is too big for its capacity" (Ashfield and de Bolla 1996, 62).

According to Addison, one finds instances of greatness in nature and occasionally in some works of architecture, so that one may first think that the sublime originates in the object. He nevertheless continues to say that, if the idea of the sublime is rooted in sense perception, things become sublime through the work of the imagination (Ashfield and de Bolla 1996, 66).

Yet, the poetic imagination fed by the sight of grand natural phenomena likely conceives two passions: terror and pity. Addison notes that, if these passions may be "unpleasant at all other times," they are "very agreeable when excited by proper descriptions" (Ashfield and de Bolla 1996, 67). This sweet and sour aspect of the experience of terror will become a common *topos* with Addison and among later writers on the subject.

Concerning the objects proper to experience of terror, Addison lists mountains, deserts, and ocean. The latter seems to occupy a prominent position

> Of all objects that I have ever seen, there is none which affects my imagination so much as the sea or ocean. I cannot see the heavings of this prodigious bulk of waters, even in a calm, without a very pleasing astonishment; but when it is worked up in a tempest, so that the horizon on every side is nothing but foaming billows and floating mountains, it is impossible to describe the agreeable horror that rises from such a prospect. A troubled ocean, to a man who sails upon it, is, I think, the biggest object that he can see in motion, and consequently gives his imagination one of the highest kinds of pleasure that can arise from greatness. I must confess, it is impossible for me to survey this world of fluid matter,

without thinking on the hand that first poured it out, and made a proper channel for its reception. Such an object naturally raises in my thoughts the idea of an almighty being, and convinces me of his existence, as much as a metaphysical demonstration. The imagination prompts the understanding, and by the greatness of the sensible object, produces in it the idea of a being who is neither circumscribed by time nor space. (Ashfield and de Bolla 1996, 69)

To summarize, from Addison the question of the sublime starts drifting away from rhetoric toward aesthetics as it becomes definitely related to nature. Beginning with Dennis, one perceives an emerging distinction between the beautiful and the sublime. Finally, Addison launches a movement toward a psychological study of the effect of the grand and terrible.

In his *Essay on the Sublime*, published posthumously in 1747, the dramatist and essayist John Baillie (d. 1743) first approached the sublime in writing from a conventional angle, as if "it were painting to the imagination what nature herself offers to the senses." He is not original, as he defines the sublime as "every thing which thus raises the mind to fits of greatness, and disposes it to soar above her mother earth; hence arises that exultation and pride which the mind ever feels from the consciousness of its own vastness." As his predecessors Dennis and Addison, he lists the vast rivers, the oceans, and the mountains as producing the elevation that eventually leads to the sublime. Things become interesting as he expands an insight already found in Richard Blackmore about novelty as a necessary condition for the sublime (Ashfield and de Bolla 1996, 41).

With Baillie, this principle of the novelty of an object is expanded into something that strongly resembles Ferdinand de Saussure's (1969, 163–65) concept of *différence*: in order to elicit the sublime, not only must objects be uncommon, but they must also be different from their surroundings.[2] For instance, a mountain is remarkable partly because it is surrounded by not-mountain. Connections with Saussurian theory go even deeper in Baillie, as he also suggests that certain objects become sublime because of their associations with other objects (Ashfield and de Bolla 1996, 98). He gives the example of certain columns whose significance as pillars comes from their contribution to the strength of the building, while the signifi-

---

2. Baillie comments that "admiration, a passion attending the sublime, ... constantly decays as the object becomes more and more familiar" (Ashfield and de Bolla 1996, 91).

cance of a freestanding column, for instance, the *colonne Vendôme*, is different because of its position.

Baillie's insight about the sublime by association will be further developed by Joseph Priestly in his *Course of Lectures on Oratory and Criticism* (1777), which theorizes that objects may take on new qualities through association, the means of this association being essentially discursive. Hence, the transfer of sublimity from one thing to another or from one experience to another is effectuated by language that transgresses boundaries. Consequently, anything, even a dunghill, to use an example from Addison (Ashfield and de Bolla 1996, 61), may be raised to the quality of sublime.

The next work radically pursues the insights found in Dennis, Addison, and Baillie. *A Philosophical Enquiry into the Origins of Our Ideas of the Sublime and the Beautiful*, by Edmund Burke (1729–1797), was first published anonymously in 1757. Early on in the book, Burke (2008, 36) defines the sublime as "whatever is in any sort terrible, or conversant with terrible objects, or operates in a manner analogous to terror." The first part of this definition gives the impression of locating the sublime in the object, while the second part seems to locate it in the subject's mind. In fact, the ambiguity of that definition reflects the ambiguity of the whole essay: although Burke's work never states that the sublime is an effect of the language, its discourse portends to enunciate that possibility.

Using the example of the ocean to explain how the sublime operates, Burke affirms that whenever the eye contemplates an immense object, its capacity is forced to such a limit in all its parts that it reaches the threshold of pain and must therefore, as the only possible way out, produce the idea of sublime (Burke 2008, 124–25). In other words, the dilation of the pupil produces the idea of the sublime at the condition of being located at an adequate distance from the object. Otherwise, if danger and pain press too much upon the subject, terror is the only emotion experienced (36–37). Other experiences that provoke terror have an influx on the whole nervous system, which contracts. From that contraction results the idea of the sublime (119–22).

Burke's description of the sublime differs in many regards from those produced by his predecessors. First, he is so immersed in the empiricist current of his time that his work resembles a treatise of experimental psychology. Second, if Burke borrows from his predecessors the idea that the terrible aspects of nature can lead to the sublime and that the sublime can be considered as a negative or painful pleasure, he is the first to make it equivalent to terror: "Indeed terror is in all cases whatsoever, either more openly or latently the ruling principle of the sublime" (2008, 54). Third, because of Burke's emphasis on terror, the sublime has become a category totally distinct from the beautiful (113–14).

Burke's attention to the mental process that takes place in the experience of the sublime may be his most important contribution, as it definitely moves the discussion away from the object to focus it on the subject, as Kant will do as well. The downside of that shift is that if, in the experience of the sublime, the mind becomes entirely full of the object, the object has simply ceased to exist.

These few pages on the question of the sublime in eighteenth-century Great Britain may indicate that it had become an all-inclusive category for those aesthetic experiences that did not fit in the catalogue of the neoclassical canon. With Burke's *Enquiry*, even the ugly could take its place as an aesthetic topic.

4. THE *CRITIQUE OF THE POWER OF JUDGMENT*, BY IMMANUEL KANT

Immanuel Kant occupies a prominent position in the study of the notion of sublime in the West. As Burke before him—from whom he borrows much—Kant attempts to describe the mental process that leads to the sublime. Subsequent works will often consist of rereadings of Kant's third critique, as, for instance, in the case of Jacques Derrida's *La vérité en peinture* (1978) and Jean-François Lyotard's *Leçons sur l'analytique du sublime* (1991).

Kant deals with the question of the sublime in his *Critique of the Power of Judgment* (1790), published after the *Critique of Pure Reason* (1781) and the *Critique of Practical Reason* (1788). In this third critique, Kant addresses the difficult question of aesthetic judgments. These represent a tough test for his theory formulated in the *Critique of Pure Reason*, according to which certain things known to human beings do not originate from the senses but come from the structure of the human mind. This kind of knowledge represents a universal corpus available a priori. Kant affirms that aesthetic judgments are to be included in that corpus. For instance, a statement such as "this flower is beautiful" can pretend to universal value because of the structure of the human mind.

The *Critique of the Power of Judgment* mostly deals with the phenomenon of the beautiful and only includes in an appendix a short section on the sublime (§§ 23–29). It may be appropriate to spend a moment on

Kant's description of beauty and of its evaluation in order to understand how he perceives the sublime.

One may observe that with Kant the aesthetic judgment is a narrow category that has little to do with aesthetic judgments made in daily life. Thus, the judgment of pure beauty assumes that the subject, namely, the self, approaches the object utterly disinterestedly, that is, without any consideration in regard to its functions or the advantages that it may provide. In such a context, a sports car or a garment cannot be qualified as beautiful—even less a person. Buildings such as churches, palaces, arsenals, and garden houses exhibit their functions so much that they cannot be the object of a pure judgment of beauty (Kant 2000, 230). Things such as flowers, some birds, some sea creatures, wandering spiral figures, and abstract wallpaper designs qualify for a judgment of pure beauty, since their respective purposes are either not obvious or not immediately pressing (229). In addition, the pure judgment of beauty should be insensitive to sensory charms that emanate from the object, for these short-circuit the universal aspect of that judgment (223–26). For example, the colorful parrot cannot be qualified as beautiful because of its colors, which could seem horrible to someone. If I estimate that the parrot is beautiful, it is because of its harmonious forms. The judgment of pure beauty is therefore a purely rational and disinterested judgment. If that judgment is rational, reason does not try to expand its knowledge but only to experience pleasure (222).

Because of the characteristics of the judgment of pure beauty, Kant puts the sublime in a different category. Indeed, if some objects are considered beautiful, it is because of their harmonious forms. In contrast, the sublime may arise from indistinct or even disproportionate objects. Mostly, however, at the difference of the judgment of pure beauty, emotions contribute much to the experience of the sublime, and reason initially proves to be unable to digest the phenomenon submitted to its attention. Kant affirms that, if the faculties of imagination, understanding, and reason operate together in a judgment of pure beauty, imagination conflicts with the faculties of understanding and reason in the case of the sublime (Kant 2000, 257). That conflict explains why the experience of the sublime often comes with a certain displeasure.

In continuity with the British tradition and especially with Burke's work, Kant holds that the experience of the sublime originates from large-size phenomena. Besides, he defines the sublime as whatever "in comparison with which everything else is small" (Kant 2000, 250). He uses examples common in British works on the sublime, such as a sea storm, a mountain range, and volcanoes, to which he adds St. Peter's church in Rome and the Egyptian pyramids.

The Kantian sublime operates in two moments. At first, the imagination is unable to embrace such large objects and feels powerless and fearful. This is a moment of displeasure. In a second moment, reason prevails and provides the means to withstand the power of large objects and the fear that they cause. That moment makes it possible to experience the power of reason over every natural object. It brings a pleasurable feeling. At this point, Kant is not far from Burke. He even endorses Burke's presupposition that the subject must be at a safe distance from the object to make possible the experience of the sublime. Otherwise, terror takes over (Kant 2000, 252, 261). Burke explained the ultimately pleasurable aspect of the sublime by the satisfaction of surviving the encounter with a large object. By contrast, Kant explains that pleasure by the capacity of the sublime to connect oneself with one's supersensible faculty.

> Nothing that can be an object of the senses is … to be called sublime. But just because there is in our imagination a striving to advance to the infinite, while in our reason there lies a claim to absolute totality, as to a real idea, the very inadequacy of our faculty for estimating the magnitude of things of the sensible work awakens the feeling of a supersensible faculty in us; and the use that the power of judgment naturally makes in behalf of the latter (feeling), though not the object of the senses is absolutely great, while in contrast to it any other is small. (Kant 2000, 250)

The latter aspect makes Kant's approach to the sublime attractive when reading the Gospels, as it describes how the experience of the sublime opens to transcendence. In addition, as Kirk Pillow (2000, 5) suggests, Kant's approach may help to deal with situations where the interpreter may grasp the whole context of a Gospel but still has difficulty making sense of the "uncanny" particular of some passages.

5. From Natural Phenomenon to Text

Most approaches to the sublime described above, with the exception of Longinus, assume that it is initially prompted by a natural phenomenon. However, I attempt a reading of two passages of Luke from the perspective of the sublime; that is, I suggest that the experience of the sublime may be prompted by a text rather than a natural phenomenon.

This proposition is theoretically possible if one accepts with Addison, Baillie, Burke, and Kant that the sublime takes place in the subject's mind rather than being a property of some phenomenon. In that regard, if the experience of the sublime is prompted by some phenomenon, nothing obliges this phenomenon to be a natural one. It can be a text, a painting, a piece of music, or some kind of human activity. Ultimately, we are always dealing with texts. As affirms Derrida (1967, 3): "il n'y a pas de hors-texte."[3] Indeed, one has to put words on one's experience to express it even though these words never leave the mind. These words belong to a language and follow the rules of that language.

A tension has nevertheless remained in the discussion from Longinus until now about the interplay between object and subject. One may ask whether every object may prompt the experience of the sublime. Indeed, one notices that thinkers on the subject tend to bring the same objects to the fore as having the capacity to induce that kind of experience: oceans, mountain ranges, volcanoes. I would add that in daily life, natural phenomena found in the Americas such as Iguazu Falls, Niagara Falls, Death Valley, and the Grand Canyon almost unanimously provoke awe among visitors. Some objects or situations may therefore be more proper to induce the experience of the sublime.

One also notices that some individuals seem insensitive to such objects. That may be due to reasons such as a lack of awareness in regard to the surrounding world or extended exposure to such phenomena.

A second roadblock is the diversity of approaches to the sublime from Longinus to Kant and the difficulty of applying one of these models or all these models to the reading of two passages from Luke. As I mentioned in the introduction of this paper, I consider the notion of the sublime heuristically, that is, as a set of lenses to perceive aspects of these passages that I could not see otherwise. More prosaically, I could say that the insights of Longinus, Dennis, Addison, Baillie, and Kant are as many wrenches, screwdrivers, sockets, planes, and cutters in my toolbox. I intend to use them eclectically as intuitions rather than trying to force a passage into a Kantian framework, for example.

---

3. Often translated as "There is nothing outside of the text."

6. Reading the Stilling of the Storm (Luke 8:22–25) and the Transfiguration (Luke 9:28–36) from a Perspective of the Sublime

Luke 8:22–25: 22 One day he got into a boat with his disciples, and he said to them, "Let us go across to the other side of the lake." So they put out, 23 and while they were sailing he fell asleep. A windstorm swept down on the lake, and the boat was filling with water, and they were in danger. 24 They went to him and woke him up, shouting, "Master, Master, we are perishing!" And he woke up and rebuked the wind and the raging waves; they ceased, and there was a calm. 25 He said to them, "Where is your faith?" They were afraid and amazed, and said to one another, "Who then is this, that he commands even the winds and the water, and they obey him?" (NRSV)

Luke 9:28–36: 28 Now about eight days after these sayings Jesus took with him Peter and John and James, and went up on the mountain to pray. 29 And while he was praying, the appearance of his face changed, and his clothes became dazzling white. 30 Suddenly they saw two men, Moses and Elijah, talking to him. 31 They appeared in glory and were speaking of his departure, which he was about to accomplish at Jerusalem. 32 Now Peter and his companions were weighed down with sleep; but since they had stayed awake, they saw his glory and the two men who stood with him. 33 Just as they were leaving him, Peter said to Jesus, "Master, it is good for us to be here; let us make three dwellings, one for you, one for Moses, and one for Elijah"—not knowing what he said. 34 While he was saying this, a cloud came and overshadowed them; and they were terrified as they entered the cloud. 35 Then from the cloud came a voice that said, "This is my Son, my Chosen; listen to him!" 36 When the voice had spoken, Jesus was found alone. And they kept silent and in those days told no one any of the things they had seen. (NRSV)

Various passages from Luke may provide various types of experiences to the reader. Borrowing terms from Daniel Patte, Monya A. Stubbs, Justin S. Ukpong, and Revelation E. Velunta, we can say that the genealogy found in Luke 3:23–37 provides a sort of "family album" experience; Jesus's response to John's emissaries (7:18–23) conveys what the "good news" is, while the parable of Lazarus and the rich man (16:19–31) may be read as a "canon," that is, as a way to assess one's behavior. Luke 8:22–25; 9:28–36 may provide an experience that might be labeled a "Holy Bible" or "goose bumps" experience (Patte et al. 2003, 27–28). Ethical aspects, ordinarily so present in Luke, are not obvious here.

As I focus on the stories of the stilling of the storm and of the transfiguration, I use the following insights exposed in the previous pages: novelty difference, types of natural phenomena, sublime by association, terror and adequate distance, movement toward supersensible, and style.

Both the stilling of the storm and the transfiguration take place in particular spatial settings: at sea and on a mountain top. Such settings are uncommon in Luke, as most of the action takes place on flat land: on the road, in someone's house, in towns and villages, in the open country, or at Jerusalem. Even though the draught of fish takes place at sea (5:1–10), there is no mention of any turbulence on the lake, and the shore never seems to be very far.[4] As one perceives, the immediate literary context of the stilling of the storm makes it stand out because of its spatial setting, the type of event, and the disciples' reaction to it. In other words, it is different from its surroundings and for that reason has one of the qualities that make possible the experience of the sublime as Baillie had remarked. It nevertheless cannot pretend to novelty under all aspects, given the previous episode of the draught of fish (5:1–10). The same thing can be said of the transfiguration. Its spatial setting makes it stand apart, but the voice from heavens has previously spoken at Jesus's baptism (3:22). There is therefore difference, but not necessarily novelty. Still, one may assume that the reader has not been overwhelmed with similar settings and events, so they still have a certain element of novelty.

As mentioned previously, eighteenth-century literature on the sublime tends to list over and over the same phenomena or places as apt to induce an experience of the sublime, among which are oceans, especially raging ones, and mountains. In the first case, the action takes place on a raging sea, while the second story takes place on a mountaintop. Could these settings send a signal to the reader about a potential experience of the sublime?

Yet these spatial settings are used very differently, depending on the stories. In the case of the stilling of the storm, the raging sea fills the whole picture. It is described economically, but with a significant number of words in proportion to the rest of the story: "A windstorm swept down on the lake, and the boat was filling with water, and they were in danger" (23b); "the wind and the raging waves" (24b); "the winds and the water"

---

4. This episode also has Peter and his companions experience awe before Jesus, as is the case with the stilling of the storm.

(25b). In several episodes where Jesus is present, much attention is given to Jesus' words and deeds and to the other protagonists' words and deeds. In the case of the stilling of the storm, the raging sea qualifies as a protagonist and gets as many lines as Jesus does. In addition, it is responsible for the disciples' emotions and is the thing on which Jesus acts. In the case of the transfiguration, the mountain setting is soberly mentioned in the first verse of the pericope and does not appear to cause any special emotion among the characters of the episode. It therefore does not induce any specific experience for the characters.

It is rather by intertextual association that the mountain setting becomes meaningful and signals an exceptional experience. As Joel Green (1997, 377–78) remarks, in addition to the mountain setting, the presence of companions, Jesus' change of appearance, the reference to the tents, the cloud, the motif of fear, and the summary of Jesus' conversation with Moses (and Elijah) about an exodus point toward a connection of the episode of the transfiguration with Exod 24–34. Similarly, the mountain setting and the presence of Elijah in the transfiguration account recall God's passage before the latter on Mount Horeb (1 Kgs 19). Not only are these episodes comparable to the one that takes place in the transfiguration, but they are also episodes that may qualify as sublime on their own, considering the awe that accompanies them and the extreme aspects of the events and characters' emotions. By sharing a common spatial setting, common characters, common events, and common emotions, the transfiguration reverberates and partakes in the sublime of such episodes.

Similarly, the spatial setting of the stilling of the storm, the raging sea, the emotions it provokes, and the final calm sea associate this episode with stories such as the passage of the Red Sea (Exod 14) and the storm at sea in the book of Jonah (Jonah 1). Such stories have struck the imagination of generations of believers.

The eighteenth century British tradition on the sublime was fascinated with the terror that made the first moment of the experience of the sublime. As explained in the previous pages, Burke even reduced the whole experience to a successful overcoming of the terror caused by a phenomenon. As he treated the dynamic sublime, Kant partly endorsed the British tradition. Interestingly, both Burke and Kant insist that the distance from the object must be adequate in order to experience the sublime. If too close, the viewer will have no chance to overcome terror. The disciples experience a strong fear that may be assimilated to terror both in the stilling of the storm and in the transfiguration. In addition, they seem never to overcome this fear. The account of the stilling of the storm portrays them still afraid at the end of the story, while the end of the transfiguration account mentions the disciples' enduring mutism. Besides, from the manner in which the story is told, one gets the impression that the disciples are unable, from the narrator's point of view, to react to the events appropriately. The stilling of the storm ends with an unanswered question that expresses their perplexity. In the transfiguration account, the narrator explicitly comments that Peter's suggestion is inadequate: "not knowing what he said" (9:33). I suggest here that from Burke and/or Kant's point of view, the disciples may be too close to the events to be able to experience them as sublime. They experience the painful first moment without, from the Kantian point of view, having the necessary narrative space for their supersensible faculty to undergo the second pleasurable moment that characterizes the experience of the sublime.

The reader is in a different position. Through the imagination, the reader has reconstituted much of the scenes, may have sat in the boat with the disciples, may have felt it rocking dangerously, and may have experienced some of their fear and impatience before the sleeping Jesus. Through the imagination also, the reader may have climbed the mountain with Jesus and the three disciples, may have decided that the moment was too important to take a nap, as do the disciples, may have experienced amazement before Jesus' face and garment, before the presence of Moses and Elijah, and before the voice from heavens. The challenge put to the reader's imagination is to portray simultaneously or in a very short span of narrative time Jesus' alternate face, his shining garment, the presence of Moses and Elijah, their conversation with Jesus, the disciples' initial nap and their waking up, Peter's suggestion, the arrival of the cloud, and the voice from the cloud. As a result, the reader's imagination is put to work, even stretched to its maximum to encompass not only unusual events but also to contain all these at the same moment in the imagination. Still, if the reader has the capacity to experience some emotions from the story and to exercise her or his imagination, the reader's position is risk free. In addition, this position gives the reader a point of view on the whole plot and therefore allows the necessary narrative space and real time to experience the second moment, which leads the reader to perceive these episodes as sublime by overcoming initial disagreeable emotions and moving into a sublime experience of transcendence.

Longinus had made a compelling case about the literary style that conveys the sublime. Even if some early eighteenth-century British thinkers, such as Dennis, first approach the sublime from the angle of poetry, Boileau may have been his only true disciple in that regard. In the present case, it is difficult to know how literary style works to convey that experience. Indeed, I have been using an English translation of a Greek text. A translation is a rewriting of a text: it changes its rhythm, its assonances, and its semantic connections. Should a study of the style in regard to the sublime be done from the Greek text or from a translation? If from a translation, why this one? Second, I have chosen, rather arbitrarily, the Lukan account of the stilling of the storm and of the transfiguration. Matthew and Mark each tell these stories differently. By comparing these accounts to each other, I might, for instance, decide that the style of the Matthean account is more apt to convey the sublime, while the Markan account of the transfiguration does a better job in the transfiguration account. Can I be that eclectic? Because of these roadblocks, my remarks from the New Revised Standard Version translation of the Lukan account are fairly general and focus on the contrasting aspects present in each account. Indeed, Longinus and his followers noticed that the human mind experiences the sublime through extreme conditions. As one examines the Lukan accounts of the stilling of the storm and of the transfiguration, one realizes that they are drawn with sharp contrasts. These accentuate their "extreme" aspects. Thus, in the account of the stilling of the storm, because of the strong wind, the sea reaches such a level of turbulence that the disciples fear for their lives (Luke 8:24). To this extreme agitation succeeds an absolute calm once Jesus has spoken. The story of the transfiguration also plays with sharp contrasts: Jesus' clothes become dazzling white (8:29); a voice from heavens is heard, but in contrast to that voice, the disciples observe a silence that sounds absolute considering the pleonastic clauses: "And they kept silent and … told no one any of the things they had seen" (8:36).

7. Conclusion

The category of the sublime has a long and rich history in the West that coincides with the redaction of the New Testament writings. It offers a different set of lenses, aesthetic in nature, to look, enjoy, and profit from passages of the Gospels such as the Lukan accounts of the stilling of the storm and the transfiguration. With further work to include, for example, the perspectives of Georg W. F. Hegel, Arthur Schopenhauer, Derrida, and Lyotard on the sublime, the toolbox displayed here could be refined and updated, especially in regard to the relationship between the sublime and the beautiful. Finally, to prove its validity, the approach will need to be tried on other passages from biblical literature.

Works Cited

Ashfield, Andrew, and Peter de Bolla, eds. 1996. *The Sublime: A Reader in British Eighteenth-Century Aesthetic Theory*. Cambridge: Cambridge University Press.

Boileau-Despréaux, Nicolas. 1674. *Oeuvres diverses du Sieur D***: avec le Traité du sublime ou du merveilleux dans le discours: traduit du grec de Longin*. Paris: Chez Denis Thierry.

Burke, Edmund. 2008. *A Philosophical Enquiry into the Sublime and Beautiful*. Edited with an introduction and notes by James T. Boulton. Routledge Classics. London: Routledge.

Derrida, Jacques. 1967. *De la grammatologie*. Collection "Critique." Paris: Minuit.

———. *La vérité en peinture*. 1978. Champ Philosophique. Paris: Flammarion.

Green, Joel B. 1997. *The Gospel of Luke*. NICNT. Grand Rapids: Eerdmans.

Kant, Immanuel. 2000. *Critique of the Power of Judgment*. Edited by Paul Guyer. Translated by Paul Guyer and Eric Matthews. The Cambridge Edition of the Works of Immanuel Kant. New York: Cambridge University Press.

Longinus. 1995. *On the Sublime*. Edited and translated by W. Hamilton Fyfe. Revised by Donald Russell. LCL 199. Cambridge: Harvard University Press.

Lyotard, Jean-François. 1991. *Leçons sur l'analytique du sublime (Kant, Critique de la faculté de juger, §§23–29)*. La Philosophie en Effet. Paris: Galilée.

Monk, Samuel H. 1960. *The Sublime: A Study of Critical Theories in XVIII-Century England with a New Preface*. 2nd ed. AA 40. Ann Arbor: University of Michigan Press.

Patte, Daniel, Monya A. Stubbs, Justin S. Ukpong, and Revelation E. Velunta. 2003. *The Gospel of Matthew: A Contextual Introduction for Group Study*. Nashville: Abingdon.

Pillow, Kirk. 2000. *Sublime Understanding: Aesthetic Reflection in Kant and Hegel*. Studies in Contemporary German Social Thought. Cambridge: MIT Press.

Saussure, Ferdinand de. 1969. *Cours de linguistique générale*. Edited by Tullio de Mauro. Prepared by Charles Bally, Albert Séchehaye, and Albert Riedlinger. Postface by Louis-Jean Calvet. Grande Bibliothèque Payot. Paris: Payot.

The Sublime Art of Prophetic Seeing: Aesthetics and the Word in the Book of Jeremiah*

Mark Brummitt

Few readers would consider the book of Jeremiah beautiful; any artistry that the individual oracles boast seems to have been betrayed by the sum of the parts. Thus, while John Bright (1965, lvi) commends the "surpassing beauty" of Jeremiah's poetry, he deems the book as a whole a "hopeless hodgepodge."[1] Given that the classic definitions of beauty emphasize order and harmony, it would seem the least-promising category for engaging the book as a whole. This is not to say that Jeremiah resists all aesthetic approaches; it is perhaps now more possible than ever to appreciate the merits of disorder—following a century during which the value ascribed beauty thus defined has declined. Jeremiah is the extreme example of a tendency in prophetic literature where all not only seems chaos but, as Abraham Heschel (1962, 10) famously characterized it, tuned "one octave too high." As a result, the reader is not drawn in by calm and melody but assaulted by violent imagery and cacophony, the often-overwhelming piling up of indictment upon indictment, metaphor upon metaphor, making wholly understandable Robert P. Carroll's (1999, 433, 438–39) provocative remark that he refuses not to be confused by Jeremiah, as if to do so is to betray an important effect.

It is precisely these features that suggest that a better descriptor than the beautiful for Jeremiah might be the *sublime*: a category indicating, somewhat paradoxically, that which exceeds representation and so grasp.

---

* This paper was first presented at the Annual Meeting of the Society of Biblical Literature, San Francisco, 20 November 2011.

1. "No sooner has he grasped a line of thought," writes Bright (1965, lvi), "and prided himself that he is following tolerably well, than it breaks off and something quite different is being discussed."

While for obvious reasons this definition may seem less than propitious as a hermeneutical device, it need not be taken as a counsel against interpretation, quite; in the context of Jeremiah, it is precisely this paradox that resonates with its peculiar encounter with the sacred in the very loss of sacred symbols. This resonates, too, with the work of the twentieth-century British painter Francis Bacon, who produced work with an eye on the biblical, or, more particularly, on the iconography of the sacred from Scripture. While Bacon, to my knowledge, made no direct reference to Jeremiah, he, as Rina Arya (2008, 59) writes, occupied a position "outside the institutions of religion and yet remain[ing] fascinated by the images.... They [Bacon and Georges Bataille] are only able to express their disillusionment through continual reference to that tradition." Bacon, she notes, expressed a particular a-theology by honing in on the violence within the sacred in isolation from any ritual buffer—a buffer that effectively shields the observer from the implications of the "real presence" (59–60). Arya suggests that Bacon takes "the reader/viewer to the holiest of profanations, where the sacred is recovered in the profane" (60), and Bacon, I propose, offers provocative ways in which to think about the affective and fetishistic functions of body imagery in Jeremiah and quite possibly new ways of identifying the sacred there, too.

More typically, however, the sublime is contrasted with the beautiful, when the latter category is used to identify something demonstrating both poise and balance and the former, the sublime, is used to denote that which disrupts these by dint of magnitude and power: the lofty mountain, the crashing waves. While the sublime can be compelling—irresistible, even—it is encountered specifically when the object somehow exceeds both representation and grasp. It is thus defined precisely in failure: in the breakdown of either expression (as in Immanuel Kant's category of a dynamical sublime [2000, §28]) or conceptualization (as in Kant's mathematical sublime [2000, §25]), a breakdown that is its distinguishing mark.

When encountered in terms of power, for example, as the dynamical sublime, the imagination is overwhelmed by a sense of force that outruns representation. In Thomas Weiskel's semiotic rearticulation of this concept, it is identified as the effect of a surplus of signified on the imagination that can find no signifier suitable to express it. "Overwelmed by meaning," Weiskel (1976, 29) writes, "the mind recovers by displacing its excess of signified into a dimension of contiguity which may be spatial or temporal." In other words, the sense of force is dispersed via ecstasies of grandeur or the idea of "something evermore about to be," as William Wordsworth

("Prelude" 6.542) expresses his imaginative encounter with an apocalyptic power ordinarily known as the Swiss Alps.

Alternatively, when experienced in relation to magnitude (Kant's mathematical sublime), it is the sheer scale or complexity of an object that defeats imagination; this is the sublime of the signifier, as Weiskel has it, in which comprehension is defeated by apprehension, by the accumulation of stimuli that cannot be contained. The result is a loss of contiguity of the kind found in John Keats's *On Seeing the Elgin Marbles*, in which the sheer scale of what he encounters seems to leave the poet unable to conceptualize them other than in "fragmentary images and shards of broken syntax" (Shaw 2006, 3), a tongue-tied response to the "shadow of a magnitude" (Keats 1950, 791). In this case, writes Weiskel (1976, 28), "the absence of a signified itself assumes the status of a signifier, disposing us to feel that behind this newly significant absence lurks a newly discovered presence."

Weiskel dubs this a "'reader's' sublime," recognizing the hermeneutical role played by reason in converting lack into a content.[2] Relating this to strategies within the prophetical texts themselves, Herbert Marks distinguishes between tautology and negation. Tautology refers to those moments, such as we find in Hab 2,[3] in which the prophet is charged to await the coming of a vision where conveyance alone is the content of what is being conveyed. The far more common strategy of *negation* refers to the "prophetic stammer," those occasions where speech seems ill-able or unfit to give an account of an encounter: the slow tongue of Moses, the unclean lips of Isaiah, and the mutism of Ezekiel are the examples he cites (Marks 1990, 62–63).

We find something akin to Herbert Marks's tautology in the first of the two vision interpretations in the first chapter of Jeremiah: the strangely empty "I am watching over my word to perform it" (1:12), uttered, of course, before any course of action has yet been declared. A negation is dramatized only a few verses earlier when Jeremiah demurs on account of his youth, a counterpart to the aphasia of his peers and,

---

2. To summarize Kant's argument: what imagination cannot represent or understanding encompass, the reason, which is autonomous/independent of nature, must compensate for. For example, when the imagination cannot represent the scale of the universe as an object available to understanding, reason compensates with the idea that the universe is infinitely great.

3. "Write the vision…. For there is still a vision…. If it seems to tarry, wait for it" (Hab 2:2–3). Unless otherwise noted, all biblical quotations are from the NRSV.

in particular, Moses. But these examples also seem equally indicative of Weiskel's "excess of signified" in which even the most inconsequential of signifiers seems to be outrun by the proliferation of meanings with the observer in the midst of them tongue-tied and sensing himself or herself threatened by the possibility of being engulfed.

Prompted by Wordsworth's tendency to encounter eternity in the decaying stumps of trees, Weiskel dubs this the *poet's* sublime. It could equally as well be dubbed a *prophet's* sublime, since this seems precisely to be what Jeremiah is commissioned to do: synaesthetically to encounter the objects of sight and sound as endlessly outweighed by excessive meanings: an almond branch for the incoming word, the spill of a tilted pot flooding all that follows in disaster.

The prophet himself becomes the locus of proliferating meanings. Aware also, perhaps, that the so-called call to celibacy in Jer 16, "You shall not take a wife nor shall you have sons and daughters in this place," marks the cessation of a flesh-and-blood line in favor of a prophetical one, the prophet's own person becomes a signifier outweighed by an excess of signified. Thus, while the book noted among the Prophets for its unusual share of biographical detail foregrounds the person of the prophet, it effectively depersonalizes him: the flesh becomes word.

In the paintings of Bacon, the body, too, is made the point of particular interest: isolated, typically, by a field of color that simultaneously conveys a claustrophobia against which the figures seem often to strain. The bodies themselves range from the clearly discernible (albeit stylized) through the considerably distorted to the merely suggested, almost faded. Thus he renders the body imprecise, unlimited, sometimes seeming to be little more than a congealed mass of meat, other times even less. Effectively, Bacon dispenses with the body-as-object in favor of the *experience* of being embodied.

This, then, is structurally comparable to the dynamical sublime, that which is identified by Weiskel with an excess of signified. It is the body-as-signifier that is here overwhelmed, this time by the sensation of being embodied. So, too, with its twisted form and smudged edges, the figure in a painting by Bacon suggests something of the displacement and dispersal that must take place when the mind is confronted with what it cannot possibly comprehend. So, taking the role given to reason in Kant's account of the sublime, the painting itself transforms unrepresentability into representation. In so doing, it also dramatizes the terror and violence suggested by the dynamical sublime. Here are torn bodies, broken boundaries, the apparent unraveling of the created order, and the distressed signifiers of signifieds that outweigh them.

Already, of course, we detect resonances with Jeremiah. The land returns to its precosmic chaos in Jer 4:23: "I looked on the earth, and lo, it was waste and void; and to the heavens, and they had no light." Typically read as a likening of military catastrophe to the end of the world, it can equally suggest the effects upon the prophetic imagination of such foreboding, the overwhelming effect of an excess of signified. In his *Philosophical Enquiry into the Origin of Our Ideas of the Sublime and the Beautiful* (1757), a major influence on Kant's own reckoning of the sublime, Edmund Burke (1990, 158) associates the sublime precisely with the terror of coming judgment. The concepts of "God, angels, devils, heaven and hell" all exceed the limits of empirical understanding (the provenance of the beautiful), yet profoundly influence the sense of a self and the world all around.

In distinguishing the sublime from the beautiful, Burke writes of the former in terms of dominance and tumescence, causing "a sort of swelling and triumph that is extremely grateful to the human mind," as he puts it in one particular passage (1990, 56). If he is oblivious to the sexualized tones of his particular conceptualization of the sublime, his predecessor by a number of centuries, Longinus, the conventional name for the author of *On the Sublime* (first or third century), is not. In his estimation, sublime speech is a practice of domination that effectively "ravishes" the listener (*Subl.* 1). Persuasion is a form of violence rather than considered conviction.

This again resonates with the language of Jeremiah: "Oh YHWH, you have enticed [פתה] me, and I was enticed; you have overpowered me, and you have prevailed" (20:7). The verb פתה, which in Exod 22:16 and Hos 2:16 indicates seduction, coupled with חזק ("overpowered") and יכל ("prevailed"), to many scholars suggests something like a rape. To others, however, it denotes trickery and deceit. By either assessment, it creates a sense of excessive coercion and abuse of divine power that within a few verses becomes the celebrated burning in his bones (20:9). The burning is perhaps Jeremiah's own version of the Bacon-like sensation of being embodied.[4] This brings us to something of a paradox, one hinted at in the work

---

4. The later cursing of the day on which he was born (20:14)—which will remind the reader of the prophet's call "before I formed you in the womb" (1:5)—effectively unites the themes of birth and death in the womb, as Louis Stulman (2005, 198) notes.

of Bacon, where, on the one hand, the body is displaced by attempts to emphasize sensation, while, on the other, it remains the essential signifying factor, not only as the origin of sensation itself but as its medium also.

In Jer 16 the prophet, as already noted, is "derealized," to use the inelegant term used by theater semioticians, to signify the termination of generations of Jerusalemites: "For thus says the LORD concerning the sons and daughters who are born in this place, and concerning the mothers who bear them and the fathers who beget them in this land: they shall die of deadly diseases" (16:2–4). While Jeremiah's body becomes a symbol or sign (ironically enough) for the termination of further generations of bodies, bodies, including that of the prophet himself, remain essential for this signifying role.

See also the recurring image of the woman in travail: "A cry as of a woman in labor, anguish as of one bringing forth her first child, the cry of daughter Zion gasping for breath, stretching out her hands, 'Woe is me! I am fainting before killers!' " (4:31). In contrast to Hosea and even Isaiah, where birthing brings forth actual children, in Jeremiah labor finally signifies only death. Again, the foregrounding of the body spells its cessation. Flesh once again yields itself to word.

In effect, this trajectory—if a brute halt can indeed be named so— attests to a radical discontinuity. The discontinuity both derealizes and yet paradoxically confirms the place of bodies in this story, primarily in their role as loci of the sublime. The radical discontinuity attested by certain texts in Jeremiah offers a challenge to the book's editorial DNA voiced in other texts, most particularly the recurring antithetical statement of plucking up and pulling down, of building and planting (1:10). The proposition is challenged by the book's own termination in exile; if planting and building goes on, it is not in the land, and Daughter Zion remains unrepaired by it.[5]

Arya effectively demonstrates how such radical disjunction functions in the work of both Bacon and Bataille. Beginning with Bacon, she compares his 1944 *Three Studies for Figures at the Base of a Crucifixion* with Matthias Grünewald's 1515 *Crucifixion*. In the latter, an altarpiece,

---

Here formation and deformation, as it were, occur in the context of an overwhelming sense of divine commission and evoke the sense of sublime terror that Burke equates with revolution and attack.

5. This places promises of return for the time being in some indefinite future Never Neverland—utopian in that they regurgitate and redeem a failed past.

which has been called an exceptional "expression of horror" (Murray and Murray 2004, 239), she notes that there is a resolution to the distortions of Christ's body through the hope and resurrection that is signaled by such elements as John the Baptist's outstretched finger. Horror and suffering are thus mitigated by the fact that they find meaning in what is coming; brokenness becomes a means toward a higher reality and new life (Arya 2009, 148).

In Bacon's work, no such hope is extended. This is signaled in the very title: *at the Base of a Crucifixion*, not *the* Crucifixion. The use of the indefinite article removes the event from the Christian narrative line. This is any crucifixion, not a particular one. Furthermore, the figures themselves are unrecognizable as any known characters traditionally placed at the foot of the cross. For Bacon, the Christian narrative betrays rather than enters into human suffering. The narrative denies the reality of suffering and suggests that it is merely something to be endured en route elsewhere. By removing the iconography from its traditional, liturgical context, Arya continues, Bacon in fact focuses attention back onto body and sensation, despite the apparent dismissal of the flesh.

At no time for Bacon is the concept of the sacred deemed irrelevant or unwelcome. The sacred is not, however, a category indicating transcendence in any traditional sense. Rather, it is proposed as a radical recognition of humanness with no escape route extended. Paradoxically, brokenness— not brokenness on the way to healing—is a locus of the presence of God.

The brokenness in Jeremiah is, in one of the book's several trajectories, final and not to be mended. New covenants such as that in 31:31–34 are not yet imagined. While this may not be the final word of the book as a whole, it does create a halt in all narratives that leaves the suffering that is represented without any clear meaning and so, in a paradoxical sense, all the more meaningful, a meaning that approximates some notions of the sublime.

In conclusion, with Jeremiah the cessation of flesh spawns a mode of reproduction by means of signification. Jeremiah exemplifies the possibility of survival as he is converted into text. But might we not also need to search for the language of new covenant in the brokenness itself, not only in the survival or healing, as Bacon has suggested? Can we search for the sacred even as it seems to attest to the absence at that moment of God?

Works Cited

Arya, Rina. 2008. A-theology and the Recovery of the Sacred in Georges Bataille and Francis Bacon. *Revue Silène*: 45–58 (English), 59–72 (French). Online: http://www.revue-silene.com/f/index.php?sp=comm&comm_id=17.

———. 2009. Remaking the Body: The Cultural Dimensions of Francis Bacon. *Journal for Cultural Research* 13:143–58.

Bright, John. 1965. *Jeremiah*. AB 21. New York: Doubleday.

Burke, Edmund. 1990. *A Philosophical Enquiry into the Origin of Our Ideas of the Sublime and Beautiful*. Introduced and edited by Adam Phillips. Oxford: Oxford University Press.

Carroll, Robert P. 1999. Something Rich and Strange: Imagining a Future of Jeremiah Studies. Pages 423–43 in *Troubling Jeremiah*. Edited by A. R. Pete Diamond, Kathleen M. O'Connor, and Louis Stulman. JSOTSup 260. Sheffield: Sheffield Academic Press.

Heschel, Abraham J. 1962. *The Prophets*. New York. Harper & Row.

Kant, Immanuel. 2000. *Critique of the Power of Judgment*. Edited by Paul Guyer. Translated by Paul Guyer and Eric Matthews. The Cambridge Edition of the Works of Immanuel Kant. New York: Cambridge University Press.

Keats, John. 1950. *English Poetry and Prose of the Romantic Movement*. Edited by George Woods. Chicago: Scott Foresman.

Longinus. 1995. *On the Sublime*. Edited and translated by W. Hamilton Fyfe. Revised by Donald Russell. LCL 199. Cambridge: Harvard University Press.

Marks, Herbert. 1990. On Prophetic Stammering. Pages 60–80 in *The Book and the Text: The Bible and Literary Theory*. Edited by Regina Schwartz. Oxford: Blackwell.

Murray, Peter, and Linda Murray. 2004. *A Dictionary of Christian Art*. Oxford Paperback References. New York: Oxford University Press.

Shaw, Philip. 2006. *The Sublime*. New Critical Idiom. London: Routledge.

Stulman, Louis. 2005. *Jeremiah*. AOTC. Nashville: Abingdon.

Weiskel, Thomas. 1976. *The Romantic Sublime: Studies in the Structure and Psychology of Transcendence*. Baltimore: John Hopkins University Press.

Wordsworth, William. 2008. *The Major Works: Including The Prelude*. Edited by Stephen Gill. Oxford's World's Classics. New York: Oxford University Press.

Perceiving Beauty in Mark 5:21–43

Antonio Portalatín

It can seem as if contemporary philosophical and literary studies have lost interest in the notion of beauty, but as Ruth Lorand (2007) affirms, "The fact that a concept is out of fashion does not make it useless or redundant"; furthermore, "beauty is as relevant now as it was in the time of Plato and of Immanuel Kant simply because it has never ceased to be of interest in everyday life." In biblical aesthetics, we observe one of the most evident rifts between academic studies and life: while there is a lack of studies on beauty in the Scriptures,[1] these texts continue to inspire artists, and in reading the Bible many people say that they have an experience of beauty, without necessarily being able to explain this phenomenon. Thus, experience prompts this study into the perception of beauty in the Bible.

With a study such as this, there are initial issues of methodology and terminology. First, the relationship of beauty and aesthetics must be clarified. Modern aesthetics separated beauty in nature from beauty found in art; aesthetics became synonymous with the study of a work of art. Thus, while Kant considers beauty both in nature and in art in his *Kritik der Urteilskraft* (1948), Georg Hegel in his *Ästhetik* (1970, 40–43) defines aesthetics as the philosophy or science of the beautiful in art. Subsequently, the *Breviario di Estetica* of Benedetto Croce (1979, 28–31) and the *Ästhetische Theorie* of Theodor Adorno (1970, 81–85), two significant aesthetic disquisitions of the past century, serve as studies on the work of art and not on beauty. In contemporary aesthetics, we can no longer call beauty

---

1. Certainly aesthetic questions have made their way into theology, and biblical texts have been studied in this regard. We observe, however, with Benedict Viviano (2008, 551): "Because theological aesthetics tended to ignore modern exegesis, modern exegesis tended to ignore it."

the sole or even the main object of aesthetics, but it remains a valid category and indeed has its place in works such as those of Croce and Adorno.

With the influence of reception theory, there emerged a second line of development that we should take into account for the concept of aesthetics. In works such as those of Hans Robert Jauss or Wolfang Iser, the emphasis moves from the study of art as the expression of the artist to that of the perception of the work of art by the subject. Iser (1994, 38) affirms that every literary work has an artistic pole (the text created by the author) and an aesthetic pole (the concretization of the text by the reader).

Thus I establish these two presuppositions for this study. First, a contemporary study of aesthetics in a New Testament text does not necessarily take beauty as its object, but beauty continues to be a legitimate category in the theoretical discourse of aesthetics. Second, beauty in aesthetics may be considered from two perspectives (never completely separated): beauty as expressed by an artist or an author, and beauty as perceived by the reader or listener of the biblical text. I will conduct my analysis from the latter position and use a constellation of concepts from Iser's aesthetic theory.[2]

1. PRINCIPLES FROM ISER

Iser's (1994, 87–89, 178) theory, called *Wirkungstheorie*, has been conceived for fiction, not for *Sachliteratur*. It is not obvious that this theory may be applied to biblical texts. One may argue, however, that the means of studying fiction are pertinent to the interpretation of biblical texts written in a genre comparable to fiction (Sonek 2009, 75). The text studied here, Mark's Gospel, qualifies as a story analogous to a work of ancient fiction. Hence, there is ground for applying Iser's reading theory to the Bible.

A general principle of Iser's theory is that every act of reading is creative and requires the use of invention and imagination. Imaginative reading does not, however, mean free reading. A reader-oriented reading, at least for Iser, differs from spontaneous interpretation according to each reader. Indeed, Iser identifies and analyzes the mechanisms that the author introduces into the text to produce a creative reading. These mechanisms allow for a guided reading; the reader engages the structures within the

---

2. Aesthetic theory is also called reception theory, reader response, or reader-oriented theory, but one should be aware that there is a variety of reception or reader theories, in addition to the distinction made by some theorists between *Rezeption* and *Wirkung* (Lategan 1989, 5). As said, I refer specifically to Iser's theory.

text, which by design lead the imagination and mind into the act of co-creating the fiction (Iser 1994, 60–61). First, in every text the writer has selected a repertoire of information comprising social and historical elements known by the reader. These elements are conventional and form meaningful groups that Iser calls *schemata* (87–142). Second, the writer organizes those elements with the help of strategies (143–74). The strategies include poetic techniques, deviation as the art of breaking expected meanings, the play between foreground and background in the narrative, the assignment of themes to segments of the text, the constant widening of the horizon of the text by the incorporation of memories and the creation of expectations, and the constitution of a system of perspectives, which include those of the narrator, the characters, the plot, and the reader. The narrator does not disappear in this reader-oriented theory, and he or she can also adopt different perspectives. One should be aware that the perspective of the narrator is only one within the series of textual perspectives found within the work; there are also those of the characters, the plot, and marked positions for the reader (162–64, 170).

The whole of the textual repertoire and strategies constitute the implied reader. Therefore, following Iser, I understand the implied reader as a set of guiding textual structures and not as an "image of the reader," whether "envisioned by the author" (Fowler 1981, 152), "created in the text" (van Iersel 1998, 17–18), or "selected by the text" (Vorster 1989, 27). Iser distinguishes the implied reader from the ideal reader, the archreader, the informed reader, and the intended reader. The implied reader is not a persona: "er verkörpert die Gesamtheit der Vororientierungen, die ein fiktionaler Text seinen möglichen Lesern als Rezeptionsbedingungen anbietet" (Iser 1994, 60).[3] In addition, the implied reader has a moving point of view (177–93), constantly changing because expectations and perspectives mutate from segment to segment of the text. Thus, the implied reader stimulates the creative activity of the real reader, because the implied reader opens possibilities, a playground (*Spielraum*; Iser 1979, 191) where the reader can react and interact with the text, imagining different alternatives to the plot but also striving to follow the direction of the text.

One important moment of the act of reading, often neglected in reader-oriented theories, is the process by which the real reader, assisted

---

3. "He embodies the entirety of the pre-directions, the conditions of reception that any fictive text has to offer to its potential readers."

by the implied reader, "synthesizes" images or pictures, since the data received from fictive texts is organized as representations (Iser 1994, 219–25).[4] These images are not simply "visual sensations" but syntheses that include elements of the repertoire and the reader's understanding of the text. Forming these images requires filling in the blanks, that is, the information not given by the author and necessary to the imagination (Iser 1994, 284–315). In addition, an image includes the affective meanings connected to it. The image is, then, the "reaction" of the reader to the present textual structures, always changing according to the moving horizon of the text. This image constitutes the aesthetic object. It is not the text alone, but the images that the reader has formed from the text.

In Iser's conception, the aesthetic object is the outcome of the reception of the artistic work, independent of its beauty. In fact, he does not deal directly with the topic of beauty. However, since I consider beauty a valid aesthetic category, in my investigation I apply Iser's theory to the perceived aesthetic object as beautiful. Iser (1994, 155) nonetheless does allude to one aspect of the theory of beauty: reading a fictive text produces pleasure. Historically, this is a constant element in the discourse on beauty, although one may debate whether pleasure constitutes an integral or accidental part of the experience of beauty. In the classical definition of beauty as an attribute depending essentially on three conditions, integrity, proportion, and radiance (Aquinas, *Sum.* 1.39.8), pleasure is also a distinctive element, to the point that Aquinas uses it to differentiate beauty from goodness (1.5.4). The philosopher of disinterest, Kant (1948, 39), rejects that pleasure be a goal of the artistic activity; nonetheless, for him pleasure or displeasure is connected to the aesthetic judgment: "das Geschmacksurteil ist ästhetisch." For others, pleasure is an essential part of the definition of beauty, as in the case of Roger Scruton (2009, 29), who affirms: "Beauty is not the source of disinterested pleasure, but simply the object of a universal interest: the interest that we have in beauty, and in the pleasure that beauty brings." I do not intend to discern the exact place of pleasure in aesthetic experience, which would demand a complete theoretical discourse, but appeal to common sense and to state that in perceiving beauty the experience of pleasure is inescapable and the fact undeniable. Thus, the beautiful images produced by the reader while reading cause pleasure,

---

4. One should observe how in a recent study of biblical beauty as that of Sonek (2009, 76), the literary character of an account is found in "artistic qualities," but there is no allusion to the creation of images.

which is both sensual and intellectual, since mind and imagination work together in their production.

2. Perceiving Beauty in Mark 5

For my aesthetic analysis, I have selected the Markan tale of the healing of the hemorrhaging woman and the resurrection of Jairus's daughter (5:21–43). This text is a Gospel narrative whose two positive conclusions contribute to a pleasurable reading, in addition to the intellectual engagement with its elaborated plot. Two difficult situations producing human pain and suffering are addressed by Jesus and find a resolution. Although both are separated cases, without directly touching each other, they are intertwined in the narration, the second story being "intercalated" (Malbon 2008, 40) or "sandwiched" (Witherington 2001, 184) within the first one. The plot advances gradually. Its beauty is closer to the quiet feeling produced by a river that flows calmly through a green prairie than to the sublime awe caused by the Niagara Falls; our task is to find the forms of quiet beauty (Wordsworth, *Lines*, 2.1) in this picture.

Structurally, the story of Mark 5:21–43 belongs to the first part of the Gospel, the ministry in Galilee, in particular relationship with the Sea of Galilee. The references to this sea begin immediately after the introductory summary of Jesus' activity (1:16) and continue until his return from Gentile territories (7:31), when the plot will be directed by the decisive turn of Peter's confession and the passion predictions to Jerusalem. The sea can be seen in some of these accounts as a theophanic motif, for instance, in the story of Jesus walking on the enraged sea (6:45–52; Gnilka 2010, 267) and probably also in the stilling of the sea storm (4:35–41). Indeed, a categorization of these narratives as mere miracle stories would fall short due to their strong revelatory significance: they pose a question about the identity of Jesus (4:41; 6:52).[5] Certainly, as Jean-François Racine (2013, 18) notes, the mighty sea has been studied as one of those places linked to the sublime, a notion explored by him in the account of the calming of the sea according to Luke (9:28–36). However, the use of this literary motif in Mark during Jesus' ministry in Galilee, with seventeen apparitions, is not limited to its occurrences with the "'extreme aspects' of the sublime (Racine 2013, 5). The sea represents splendid scenery for the first part of

---

5. See the combination of both accounts in Marcus 2000, 424–25.

the Gospel; indeed, with this element the reader will compose images of the activity of Jesus from the repertoire of the Galilean people. This visual element forms part of the structure called the implied reader that the real reader assumes and thus helps the real reader to build a meaningful image or picture.

Thus, in 5:21 the reader is informed that Jesus crossed the sea by boat and continued, presumably, his teaching activity. In the first image of this narrative, the teacher appears in the foreground with the sea in the background.[6] The reader, however, has on the horizon the memory of the stormy sea calmed down by the "divine" Jesus (4:35–41; Pss 65:8; 89:10; 107:29), this same sea where stillness now reigns. Jesus is in the center of the picture, but the established relationship with the sea completes the visual Christology of this opening, since this background forms part of the image of Jesus.[7] In addition, the whole, with this wide background, stimulates the reader to create a pleasurable and beautiful scene.

One should note that the reader is asked to fill in the rest of the blanks of the image. There is no certain physical description of Jesus that the reader should somehow supply; there are no further details of the sea and the people on the shore, excepting the fact that they were numerous. The reader has latitude and license. In addition, this is not a static image, and the reader is asked to imagine the movement of the teacher and of the people, their positions (one may imagine Jesus with his back to the sea), and other details of the shore. The narrator assumes his usual perspective in the Gospel: the omniscient one (Malbon 2008, 34), detached from the scene, and knowing more than the reader and the characters. He shows us the sea, Jesus, and the people. This strategy of omniscience will be particularly useful in this account, because it allows the narrator to enter into the inner thoughts and emotions of the characters (Murfin and Ray 2009, 355).

---

6. I prefer the reading of v. 21 with the phrase ἐν τῷ πλοίῳ. In addition to the arguments discussed by Metzger (1994, 72–73)—its presence in a great number of important manuscripts and the omission due to a scribal error or assimilation to the parallel passage Luke 8:40—one should consider that references to the boat in Mark (seventeen times) outnumber those found in Matthew (thirteen times) and Luke (eight times). To Mark, the boat belongs to the scenery of Jesus' activity in Galilee.

7. Murphy (1995, 6) speaks of "Christological imagination" and advocates for its use in theology.

Then the reader is led to a second picture that seems to interrupt the first one: while Jesus is teaching, Jairus comes, falls down before Jesus, and asks Jesus to heal his daughter (5:22–23). The whole gesture of prostration is a schema from the Jewish cultural repertoire that conveys the idea of acknowledgment of authority, not as an act of worship, but of petition (Donahue and Harrington 2002, 173). In addition, within his or her horizon, the reader has the memory of a similar gesture by a leper (1:40). However, the authorial selection of the same gesture performed by someone who has a local function and authority in the synagogue is still more eloquent. The perspective of the real reader, guided by the implied reader, focuses on Jesus while the horizon of the text moves from the former beautiful image—Jesus with the sea at the background—to this one where the reader is invited to imagine a majestic Jesus before whom an authoritative figure falls down. Indeed, the sensorial image of the natural scenery works together with the cultural schema of authority, for power influences the perception of beauty in the New Testament as well as in the Hebrew Bible (Penchansky 2013, 48).

In this image, the reader also has the opportunity to know the perspective of Jairus. Jairus speaks to Jesus and asks him to go and heal his child (v. 23). Jairus's petition is elegantly crafted, as he refers affectively to his daughter with the diminutive θυγάτριόν. He avoids the direct reference to death using a paraphrase, and he uses the sibilant sounds of the conjunctives σωθῇ and ζήσῃ to produce a sonorous play that emphasizes a deeper relationship of these words at the semantic level. The perspective of the reader is clarified to include the expectation that Jesus should go and heal that child. The diverse perspectives of the image—that of the narrator, Jairus, and the reader—concentrate on Jesus, who continues to be the focus of attraction.

Then the point of view changes again and brings the reader to the third picture, on the way to the house of Jairus. The scene is full of movement, a pleasure for the imagination: people pushing, disciples moving near Jesus (appearing suddenly in the narrative), a woman touching Jesus and hiding, and Jesus turning to see who touched him. The change of tenses in the narration from the historical present in verses 22–23 to the aorist and imperfect in verse 24 also prompts the reader to add movement to the image.[8]

---

8. I read in v. 23 with, among others, the manuscripts Sinaiticus and Alexandrinus and against Vaticanus and other manuscripts the present verbal form παρακαλεῖ. It

In this last verse, the interplay of verbs causes a dynamic picture: during the action of going, which remains in the background, people, in the foreground of the narration, are following and repeatedly pressing upon him.

In the midst of this movement, we "see" a woman who approaches Jesus from behind, touches him, and is healed. There are many visual points at which the reader should fill in the picture: the landscape; the physical positions of Jairus, the disciples, and others; the behavior of Jesus before the people and especially in reaction to the woman. This scene allows the reader to produce the imaginative aesthetic object. The frequent use of this scene in early Christian iconography, with diverse depictions, proves the point (Baert 2010, 54). When the woman approaches Jesus, the focus of the narrator shifts to the woman and introduces the reader to her perspective. First, the reading moves into her past to gain a background of her sickness (vv. 25–26), then to the present, where she is at the center of the picture (v. 27), and finally into her train of thought to apprehend her intention (v. 28).

The skilled interplay of the "register of focalizations" (Marguerat and Bourquin 1999, 75) is one of the most remarkable qualities of Mark's account of this sick woman. Presenting her perspective, the narrator uses external focalization—the reader observes the character from outside—and internal focalization—the reader knows the character's thoughts and feelings (72–74). The action of the woman is understandable within the horizon of the text, since the reader knows that sick people tried to touch Jesus to be healed (3:10). Hence, the perspective of the reader looks with the woman toward this healing, while the perspective of the plot moves toward such an outcome. Finally, the diverse perspectives (narrator, woman, reader, plot) converge in the miraculous deed. The focus remains on Jesus, who reveals himself as the thaumaturge of a miracle story.

A theological aspect of his figure is disclosed through the nature of this healing. The woman is impure due to her hemorrhages (Lev 15:25) and is not to touch anyone. Nonetheless, the reader knows from the horizon of the text that Jesus purifies people, as in the surprising healing of the leper through touch (1:40–45), without any indication that Jesus became defiled. The healing of the woman with hemorrhages completes the image of a man who in this regard is above the law or, at least, can be exempted

---

agrees with the style of the narrative, already started in the present tense in v. 22, with a vivid image of the encounter of Jairus and Jesus.

from some of its commands. For example, in Mark 1:44 Jesus sends the healed man to the priests, while in Mark 5 there is no such an action. One may argue that impurity has a minimal role in this account or none at all, as some feminist readings have suggested (Haber 2008, 133–34), but the burden of proof lies on them, since purity issues "were at the forefront of Jewish life, including early Church" (132), and Mark 5:24 evokes Lev 15. Haber explains that purity has a role in this text but that the focus is the healing story (137). This affirmation may reflect the emphasis on the sickness of the woman in the narrative, but it does not make the purity-related meaning of the healing secondary. As the miracles of the healing of the paralytic (2:1–12) and the man with a withered hand (3:1–6) had two levels of meaning, the reader knows, from the Jewish repertoire, that healing the woman with blood discharges has its legal effects. The powerful figure of Jesus in the narration proceeds not simply from his authority over nature but also from his capacity to return a woman to the legal realm of purity. Again, the implied reader is led to compose a picture of Jesus with the beauty of this majesty.

After the healing, the double use of the typical Markan adverb εὐθύς in verses 29 and 30 marks a change in perspectives: from the woman to Jesus. Now the reader imagines Jesus seeking the person who touched him, although the reader already knows her identity. The disciples' ironic remark on the naïveté of the question of Jesus underscores the particularity of the woman's touch. It does not seem that at this moment everyone was seeking healing and trying to touch Jesus. Only the woman of faith sought him (v. 34). The healing effects an unwilling flow of energy that is unexpected for the reader, since it has no precedent in the Gospel. The horizon of the text will widen, and from now on the operation of these δυνάμεις in Jesus will form part of his picture (see, e.g., 6:14). It is still more intriguing that Jesus does not know who caused the release of his powers; indeed, this fact will create the conditions for a kind of *anagnorisis* at the conclusion of the scene.[9] The concentration of "epistemological language" (Marcus 2000, 368) characterizes the text: Jesus "perceives" that the force came out from him (v. 30), the disciples answer that he "sees" the people pressing in on him (v. 31), but Jesus insists on "looking around" to "see" who had done that (v. 32), and finally, the woman "knows" (v. 33) what happened. Theological questions about the "ignorance" of Jesus add to this

9. *Anagnorisis* explains a reversal of fortune (Murfin and Ray 2009, 18).

passage (Donahue and Harrington 2002, 175).[10] This ignorance is part of the drama that grows in intensity as Jesus seeks the person who touched him, while the disciples obscure the woman until she comes forth publicly to meet Jesus.

In the next image, the reader returns to the perspective of the woman. She approaches Jesus with fear and trembling (v. 33), characteristic emotions of the human being before the divine (see LXX Exod 15:16; Deut 2:25; 11:25; Ps 2:11; Jdt 15:2). This image contains many points that are, in Iser's words, left blank. Left unsaid is what the disciples and the people are doing, and the manner in which the woman approaches Jesus is open to the imagination. Filling in these blanks, the reader is compelled to focus on the two figures and to silence the rest of the people in the scene in order to hear the dialogue. The woman is at the feet of Jesus, perhaps as a gesture of worship of God, who works through his servant Jesus. Here the narrative voice interprets the gesture of the woman (v. 33) and brings the reader to see a sort of theophany, or, we could say, Christophany. The motif of the manifestation of the glory of God is introduced. This motif is a central one in the repertoire of the aesthetics of biblical beauty (e.g., Ezek 1:4–28).[11] In the encounter of this woman with Jesus, there are no other traditional expressions of God's glory, such as splendorous light and thunderous sounds (e.g., Exod 19:16), but narration intimates feelings typically associated with a theophany. The works of God in nature and amidst the people of Israel are manifestation of the glory of God (e.g., Ps 19), and the attitude of the woman before Jesus reflects her acknowledgment of the work of God, confirmed by the words of Jesus (v. 34).

Both Jairus and the woman fall down before Jesus, and in both cases the implied reader is prompted to develop a majestic picture of Jesus. Unlike Jairus, the woman is not a figure of authority, nor is her gesture a gesture of petition. However, her gesture arguably is still greater because it responds to a theophanic moment. The reader is led to compose an image of Jesus who is not the omniscient θεὸς ἀνήρ—he did not know who

---

10. Interestingly, Marcus (2000, 359) sees in the gesture of Jesus of looking around, whose object is a woman due the feminine participle ποιήσασαν (v. 32), a revelation of his supernatural "clairvoyance," not noting a contradiction with his lack of knowledge in his previous question (v. 30).

11. Here we should refer to the concept of כבד in the Old Testament and the theological reflections of Karl Barth and Hans Urs von Balthasar. See an introduction in Viladesau 1999, 26–35.

touched him—but a still-sovereign "divine" man who can produce feelings of awe and fear.

Suddenly, while Jesus speaks to the woman, a new action begins (v. 35), and the reader is called to produce a new image. The reader supposes that Jairus has been with Jesus during the intervening action, but there is no reference to the official until someone or some people come from his house—details are left to the imagination—and announces (the narrator uses direct speech for the sake of vividness) that his daughter has died and there is no need to disturb the "teacher" (v. 35). Jesus overhears and commands Jairus "not to fear" (v. 36).[12] This expression is used here for the first time in the Gospel of Mark (see 6:50). This fear differs from that of the woman: it is not a "pious" fear but human fear before death (see 4:40). However, his imperative joined to a call to faith, the same that he found in the woman (v. 34), creates the expectation in the reader that Jesus can also resurrect dead people. The resulting image of Jesus is one of a sovereign teacher whose command denotes dominance over death or, at least, fearlessness before it.

In the next picture the reader "sees" Jesus going and entering into Jairus's house (v. 38). The omniscient narrator brings the reader into the perspective of Jesus. The complete image is composed of two groups of people. First, there is a definite and intimate group, the company of Jesus, Jairus, and three chosen disciples (with names: Peter, James, and John), whom the girl's mother will draw into the house. Then there is an undetermined number of gathered people crying and wailing according to a Jewish custom of mourning (Gnilka 2010, 127). The reader should recreate in his or her imagination this crowd to whom Jesus speaks paradoxically: the child "οὐκ ἀπέθανεν ἀλλὰ καθεύδει" (v. 39). The sonorous play of this expression with the dental sound pleases the ears and points to an ambiguity at the semantic level: the obscure border between sleeping and death.

A truly "literal" reading would require considering the girl to be sleeping. But this interpretation weakens the miraculous nature of this action; Jesus comes to do a great deed requiring faith from the daughter's father (5:36), not to clarify a mistaken diagnosis (Beavis 2010, 55). The best explanation remains in the metaphor of death as sleeping, used in

---

12. From the three possible meanings of παρακούσας, pace Gnilka 2010, 216 and Marcus 2000, 362, I prefer the first one simply because it fits best in the context: Jesus reacts to the news received (see also Bauer 1988, 1251).

mythology (e.g., the myth of Orpheus), in the Scriptures (Dan 12:2), and in the early church (Eph 5:14). Jesus will resurrect the girl as one awakens a sleeping person.

The last image of the story addresses the reader's expectation of a miracle. The reader, along with the first group, follows Jesus to the place where the child lies. The gestures and words of Jesus build the aesthetic of the scene: taking her hand and commanding her to stand up. This time he is not touched, but he touches another. Nonetheless, it is also an action that should render him impure (Num 19:11–16). However, as in the story of the woman, there is no indication of defilement, and a miracle is performed. The Aramaic words of Jesus mark the solemn moment with sonority: the reader is also a hearer who listens to the *ipsissima verba*—at least this is the fictional effect—of a powerful Jesus (see 7:34).[13] The resurrection of a dead person is the greatest of his miracles. It makes him similar to Elijah (1 Kgs 17:17–24) and Elisha (2 Kgs 4:18–37), although the tales of the prophets do not refer to powers comparable to those operating in Jesus.

In addition, it is probable that in this narrative a principle of inversion is working in relationship to the story of Jephthah's daughter (Judg 11:34–40). Both are accounts with a distinctive relationship between father and daughter, where the father has a public function and the virgin daughter is the only child (stated in Judges, implicit in Mark). Above all, the climax of both stories is related to the death that the daughter should undergo. The inversion, however, occurs in this Gospel with the introduction of the resurrection (Beavis 2010, 61–62). In Mark, "where the understanding of the resurrection of the dead is a key to understanding the significance of Jesus (9:6), the raising of Jairus' daughter is fraught with eschatological significance" (55). From the perspective of the reader, at least, the confrontation of life and death enters into the horizon of Jesus' ministry.

The aesthetic dimension provides additional support for reading the two miracles as one story. Mark's narrative artistry of combining two accounts has been extensively studied (e.g., Derrett 1982, 474–505). They are intertwined by literary motifs: twelve years (vv. 25, 42), the designation "daughter" (vv. 34, 35), the imperative of faith (vv. 34, 36). Brenda Schildgen (1998, 100–102, 104–8) relates what she calls "intercalation" to

---

13. There has been speculation of the link of Jesus' Aramaic words to magic rites of healing (Marcus 2000, 373). However, a more simple and effective explication is that, by remembering Jesus' language, the narrator reinforces the illusion of hearing Jesus himself.

the "suspended time" by which a secondary story is put in the foreground with the purpose of focusing the reader on an aspect that could help one to understand the primary story better. However, we should not totally subordinate the story of the sick woman to that of the dead girl, because it presents a complete narrative and set of images for itself. But we do observe a progression in the narrative center of both accounts, which is the image of Jesus as full of the power of God (vv. 30, 41). This is another reason to consider the second miracle as a resurrection, because the miracle of the sick woman prepares the reader to contemplate the greater miracle of the resurrection. But we do not go as far to say that healing prefigures the final resurrection, when all infirmities will be healed (Marcus 2000, 363); nevertheless, the advance from a healing to a resurrection is inherent in the structure of this narrative.

Using reception theory, we perceive beauty in Mark's story of the resurrection of Jairus's daughter and the healing of the hemorrhaging woman. We have also found reasons that account for the pleasure of reading this text. At the structural level, the harmony of the two stories intercalated and pointing toward the central character of Jesus entices the reader. Moreover, the reader finds the stylistic features—sonorous wordplays, skilled shifts of verb tenses, irony, ambiguity—placed throughout the text to embellish the narrative. Beauty appears exceptionally in the set of images and pictures that the implied reader prompts the real reader to creatively compose. The reader should re-create a magnificent background with the sea and dynamic scenes involving different characters or groups of characters (crowd, disciples, petitioners). These are stimulating images produced from diverse perspectives. In the center of these images, one "sees" the gestures of the president of the synagogue who fell down before Jesus or the woman who surreptitiously touched him. Particularly, the reader contemplates the sovereign and attractive image of Jesus, whose physical traits are left to the imagination of the reader, but they evoke those of a διδάσκαλος (5:35), or "teacher," who acts with consequences on nature and the law and causes theophanic perceptions in those who witness his power. Mark 5:21–43 is a narrative rich in theological aesthetics and replete with expressions of the beautiful.

Works Cited

Adorno, Theodor W. 1970. *Ästhetische Theorie*. Vol. 7 of *Gesammelte Schriften*. Suhrkamp Taschenbuch Wissenschaft 1707. Frankfurt: Suhrkamp.

Aquinas, Thomas. 1959. *Suma Teológica: Edición bilingüe*. Madrid: Biblioteca de Autores Cristianos.

Baert, Barbara. 2010. "Wenn ich nur sein Kleid möchte anrühren": Die Frau mit dem Blutfluss in der frühmittelalterlichen Ikonographie (Mark 5:24b–34 parr). *ZRGG* 62:52–76.

Bauer, Walter. 1988. *Griechisch-deutsches Wörterbuch zu den Schriften des Neuen-Testaments und der frühchristlichen Literatur*. Edited by Kurt Aland and Barbara Aland. 6th ed. Berlin: de Gruyter.

Beavis, Mary Ann. 2010. The Resurrection of Jephthah's Daughter: Judges 11:34–40 and Mark 5:21–24, 35–43. *CBQ* 72:46–62.

Croce, Benedetto. 1979. *Guide to Aesthetics (Breviario di Estetica)*. Translated by Patrick Romanell. South Bend, Ind.: Regnery.

Derrett, J. Duncan M. 1982. Mark's Technique: The Haemorrhaging Woman and Jairus' Daughter. *Bib* 63:474–505.

Donahue, John R., and Daniel J. Harrington. 2002. *The Gospel of Mark*. SP 2. Collegeville, Minn.: Liturgical Press.

Fowler, Robert M. 1981. *Loaves and Fishes: The Function of the Feeding Stories in the Gospel of Mark*. SBLDS 54. Chico, Calif.: Scholars Press.

Gnilka, Joachim. 2010. *Das Evangelium nach Markus*. EKKNT 2. Neukirchen-Vluyn: Neukirchener. [Orig. 1978.]

Haber, Susan. 2008. A Woman's Touch: Feminist Encounters with the Hemorrhaging Woman in Mark 5:24–34. Pages 171–92 in *"They Shall Purify Themselves": Essays on Purity in Early Judaism*. Edited by Adele Reinhartz. EJL 24. Atlanta: Society of Biblical Literature.

Hegel, Georg W. F. 1970. *Vorlesungen über Ästhetik*. Suhrkamp Taschenbuch Wissenschaft 613. Frankfurt: Suhrkamp. [Orig. 1834.]

Iersel, Bas M. F. van. 1998. *Mark: A Reader-Response Commentary*. Translated by W. H. Bisscheroux. Sheffield: Sheffield Academic Press.

Iser, Wolfang. 1979. *Der Implizite Leser: Kommunikationsformen des Romans von Bunyan bis Beckett*. UTB 163. Munich: Fink.

———. 1994. *Der Akt des Lesens: Theorie ästhetischer Wirkung*. 4th ed. UTB 636. Munich: Fink.

Kant, Immanuel. 1948. *Kritik der Urteilskraft*. Edited by Karl Vorländer. PhB 39. Leipzig: Meiner. [Orig. 1790.]

Lategan, Bernard C. 1989. Coming to Grips with the Reader in Biblical Literature. *Semeia* 48:3–17.

Lorand, Ruth. 2007. In Defense of Beauty. *Aesthetics Online*. Online: http://aesthetics-online.org/articles/index.php?articles_id=34&print=1.

Malbon, Elizabeth Struthers. 2008. Narrative Criticism: How does the Story Mean? Pages 29–57 in *Mark and Method: New Approaches in Biblical Studies*. Edited by Janice Capel Anderson and Stephen D. Moore. 2nd ed. Minneapolis: Fortress.

Marcus, Joel. 2000. *Mark 1–8*. AB 27. Garden City, N.Y.: Doubleday.

Marguerat, Daniel, and Yvan Bourquin. 1999. *How to Read Bible Stories: An Introduction to Narrative Criticism*. Translated by John Bowden. London: SCM.

Metzger, Bruce M. 1994. *A Textual Commentary on the Greek New Testament*. 2nd ed. Stuttgart: Biblia-Druck.

Murfin, Ross, and Supryia M. Ray. 2009. *The Bedford Glossary of Critical and Literary Terms*. 3rd ed. Boston: Bedford.

Murphy, Francesca Aran. 1995. *Christ the Form of Beauty: A Study in Theology and Literature*. Edinburgh: T&T Clark.

Penchansky, David. 2013. Beauty, Power, and Attraction: Aesthetics and the Hebrew Bible. Pages 47–65 in this volume.

Racine, Jean-François. 2013. The Potential of the Category of Sublime for Reading the Episodes of the Stilling of the Storm (Luke 8:22–25) and of the Transfiguration (Luke 9:28–36). Pages 5–22 in this volume.

Scruton, Roger. 2009. *Beauty*. Oxford: Oxford University Press.

Schildgen, Brenda Deen. 1998. *Crisis and Continuity: Time in the Gospel of Mark*. JSNTSup 159. Sheffield: Sheffield Academic Press.

Sonek, Krzysztof. 2009. *Truth, Beauty, and Goodness in Biblical Narratives: A Hermeneutical Study of Genesis 21:1–21*. BZAW 395. Berlin: de Gruyter.

Viladesau, Richard. 1999. *Theological Aesthetics: God in Imagination, Beauty and Art*. Oxford: Oxford University Press.

Viviano, Benedict T. 2008. The Adoration of the Magi: Matthew 2:1-23 and Theological Aesthetics. *RB* 115:546–67.

Vorster, Willen S. 1989. The Reader in the Text: Narrative Material. *Semeia* 48:21–39.

Witherington, Ben. 2001. *The Gospel of Mark: A Socio-rhetorical Commentary*. Grand Rapids: Eerdmans.

Wordsworth, William. 2012. Lines Composed a Few Miles above Tintern Abbey. In *Lyrical Ballad: The Literature Network*. Online: http://www.online-literature.com/wordsworth/lyrical-ballads. [Orig. 1798.]

BEAUTY, POWER, AND ATTRACTION:
AESTHETICS AND THE HEBREW BIBLE

David Penchansky

"One does not see anything until one sees its beauty."
— Oscar Wilde (quoted in Viladesau 1999, 9)

The Hebrew words translated as "beauty" do not carry the same meaning as the English word. Although some overlap exists, they are not the same. Western philosophers regard beauty as one of the "transcendentals," along with truth and goodness. In the Hebrew Bible, יפה and other corresponding words are more geared to physical appearance. Although the Western tradition tends to disparage the physical appearance, in the Hebrew Bible a character described as beautiful has power. I here analyze the meanings of beauty, avoiding Western categories, to explore the significance of "beauty" words within an ancient Israelite context.

1. "AH, YOU ARE BEAUTIFUL; YOUR EYES ARE DOVES." (SONG 1:15)[1]

Within ancient Israelite literature, the perception of beauty begins with the eyes. Francis Landy (1980, 82) states, "The beauty of eyes is especially interesting, for they can only unite without touching, at a psychic distance; their objective separateness is the condition for their fusion." Luke Ferretter (2004, 128) suggests that "the eyes are the features that most often contribute to human beauty in the Bible."

Of the two sisters, Leah and Rachel, "Leah's eyes were weak [ועיני לאה רכות], but Rachel was graceful and beautiful" (Gen 29:16–17). This word רכות has the sense of "delicate" or "fragile," which some have interpreted

---

1. Unless otherwise indicated, biblical quotations are from the NRSV.

as soft, pleasing, or lovely, but the story suggests rather that Leah's eyes are weak and sickly; she is squint-eyed and often bumping into things.

In several passages, the Song of Songs also expresses the beauty of the beloved's eyes:

> Ah, you are beautiful, my love;
> ah, you are beautiful;
> your eyes are doves. (1:15)

> You have ravished my heart, my sister, my bride,
> you have ravished my heart with a glance of your eyes,
> with one jewel of your necklace. (4:9)

> Turn away your eyes from me,
> for they overwhelm me! (6:5)

The experience of beauty overwhelms and ravishes the lover. There is pain in beauty. Although not mentioned explicitly in this passage, in the perception of beauty there is also loss and fear.

1.1. BEAUTY THROUGH THE LENS OF POWER

The disparity between Leah's less-attractive eyes and Rachel's beauty creates hostility between the two sisters and arranges them in a hierarchy. The narrator draws our attention to Leah's weak eyes. Rachel, in contrast, is stunning. Leah suffers from a lack of love for the rest of her life. She is desperate, consumed, and obsessed with winning her husband's affection (Hubbard 1997, 51). Lack of beauty for the woman (Leah) results in a love deficit, as Robert Hubbard calls it. The woman with less beauty receives less love in the arrangement with Jacob. Note the words of struggle: "Then Rachel said, 'With mighty wrestlings I have wrestled with my sister, and have prevailed'" (Gen 30:8). Leah said, "'now my husband will honor me, because I have borne him six sons'; so she named him Zebulon" (Gen 30:20; Hubbard 1997, 59).

Here the perception of beauty has to do with hierarchy: one human being over another in terms of privileges, status, and authority. "The impression of power is an essential part of beauty in the Hebrew Bible," observes Ferretter (2004, 128). He thereby explains why Song of Songs compares the lover to towers or fortified cities (Song 4:4; 8:10).

In David's narrative, the young man David had "beautiful eyes [יפה עינים] and was handsome [וטוב ראי]" (1 Sam 16:12). These three literary characters, David, Rachel, and Leah, compare nicely. Eyes are mentioned in the case of David and Leah, and the word יפה (beautiful) is mentioned with regard to Rachel and David. We note a complex web of power relationships regarding who has beauty and who does not. This relationship between beauty and power was understood in the earliest aesthetic debates that took place in Europe. Terry Eagleton (1990, 35), quoting the aesthetic philosopher Lord Shaftesbury (1671–1713), observes, "politics and aesthetic are deeply intertwined: to love and admire beauty is 'advantageous to social affection, and highly assistant to virtue, which is itself no other than the love of order and beauty in society.'"

Landy (1980, 57–58) focuses on those who perceive beauty in others and identifies a power dynamic there as well: "Thus Beauty is always the result of tension, between desire and control.... Hence the ambivalence of Beauty, as the object of desire. Because men project their emotions onto the source of arousal, the destructive, sadistic impulses evoked by Beauty are attributed to Beauty itself."

This is different from the notion of beauty as a quality inhering in the beautiful object, and perhaps it is an equally important perspective. Landy speaks here of beauty not from the perspective of the beautiful one but from the point of view of the one who perceives/experiences the beauty.

Both Rachel and David have beauty. That beauty enables them to gain power over their competitors. In the case of Rachel, her beauty made her the favorite of Jacob, her husband. Jacob, the patriarch, defines the terms of beauty: he is attracted to Rachel and not to Leah. He thereby, by means of this authority, exercises power over both. In the case of David, his beauty enables him to gain first the loyalty of Saul's children and then the fealty of the nobles in his plot against King Saul.

Rachel and Leah are women, and David is a man. Therefore, the dynamic of their struggle and the way beauty impinges on the lives of Rachel and Leah is entirely different than in the case of David. The women struggle over the attention of Jacob, who had four wives. These two (at least) compete for the privilege that comes with the status of favored wife. In this story, beauty trumps fertility. Even though Leah bears sons for Jacob, Rachel's beauty attracts Jacob more than Leah's active womb. The narrative suggests that Rachel's beauty gains the attention of the patriarch and affords her status in the family. The field in which the conflict between the women takes place is the household. They struggle to gain the attention of a man.

The narrator commends David to his readers as having "beautiful eyes and being handsome in appearance." However, this reference to beauty differs from that of the story of Rachel. The field upon which David's beauty operates is a much wider field, encompassing first the royal court of Saul and ultimately the entire kingdom. David's beauty gives him power over others: over Michal, over Jonathan, and over the handmaids of his servants.

One might say that Rachel's beauty gave her some power over her husband, but even then it could not afford her the status that both she and Leah agreed was paramount: the status that comes from bearing sons. Leah hoped each time that her sons would grant her the favored status and that she would win her husband's love:

> Leah conceived and bore a son, and she named him Reuben; for she said, "Because the LORD has looked on my affliction; surely now my husband will love me." She conceived again and bore a son, and said, "Because the LORD has heard that I am hated, he has given me this son also"; and she named him Simeon. Again she conceived and bore a son, and said, "Now this time my husband will be joined to me, because I have borne him three sons"; therefore he was named Levi. (Gen 29:32–34)

Rachel believed that even with her husband's love, she would not be complete without sons. However, for Jacob, Rachel's beauty made her his favorite (Hubbard 1997, 59).

Because Rachel is more beautiful than her sister Leah, she gains the love of her husband. This speaks indirectly about the tribes. These are their origin stories. Therefore, if Rachel is the sympathetic character, the tribes that come from Rachel's stock (Manasseh, Ephraim, and Benjamin) inherit the right to dominate. However, in each historical period the meaning might change. With whom does the narrator sympathize in the story? If Leah instead of Rachel is the sympathetic character (because she is treated unfairly, through no fault of her own), then we have an anti-Saul, pro-David polemic. David is indeed from the tribe of Judah, and Leah is Judah's mother. Saul is from the tribe of Benjamin, and Rachel is Benjamin's mother. But if, as I suspect, the narrator's sympathies lie with the beautiful sister Rachel, then the politics of the passage are reversed. But in either case, in the story beauty equals power.

Leah lost in the power competition against her "sister-wife," but Rachel cannot be said to have won. After many years of childlessness, she bore once but died giving birth to her second son. In contrast, David won most of his power struggles. David's beauty got him what he wanted. Neither Rachel's beauty nor Leah's fecundity gained for them their heart's desire: Rachel for children, and Leah for her husband's love. Rachel's beauty became a sign of their enmity and competition, the barrier that prevented them from supporting each other.

1.2. BEAUTY THROUGH THE LENS OF ATTRACTION

Attraction (as opposed to power) is another way to understand the perception of beauty. Beauty is not some quality in the beautiful object but rather the attraction between the perceiver and the object. Attraction here holds its most basic meaning, a drawing toward the object. The opposite of attraction is repulsion. Attraction is primal and immediate, not a result of cognition or considered judgment. Its opposite is equally strong and deep-seated. Aside from Leah, there are few references to unattractiveness or ugliness in the Bible. In Second Isaiah, there is one. The servant of Yahweh

> had no form or majesty that we should look at him, nothing in his appearance that we should desire him. He was despised and rejected by others; a man of suffering and acquainted with infirmity; and as one from whom others hide their faces he was despised. (Isa 53:2–3)

The appearance of the Servant of Yahweh revolts people and drives them away. This response is precognitive, a visceral reaction to sensory stimuli. It runs very deep. A character's "soul responses" to the beautiful or to the revolting link inextricably to her physical self. Landy observes that this attraction is always directed toward something outside, to the "Other": "Beauty can only be experienced at a distance. It is an attribute of objects, contemplated separately from oneself, preserved intact, and ineffable. Yet it is also the focus of libidinal desire, for unification, for closure" (Landy 1980, 57). This is a seminal definition of beauty, which he understands as: (1) the object of contemplation, the Other and not the self; and (2) focus of libidinal desire. There is a longing to both consume the Other but also to keep distance, to establish and maintain a separate identity.

1.3. יפה: The Key Word for Beauty

In contrast to Leah, the narrator describes Rachel as "graceful and beau-tiful" (ורחל היתה יפת-תאר ויפת מראה) (Gen 29:17), literally, "beauti-ful of form and beautiful of appearance." "Form" refers to the body, while "appearance" refers to the face. The Arabic word for beauty always means face, so to describe a beautiful body one would need explanatory adjec-tives, as here in Rachel's description. The author uses the word יפה (beau-tiful) two times in reference to the younger sister. We must stop and con-sider this word more closely. It serves as the lynchpin for any analysis of beauty in the Hebrew Bible.

In Western philosophical and theological discourse, the word "beauty" (and its equivalents) refers to human beauty, divine beauty, and natural beauty. However, the ancient Israelites had two entirely different categories of what might be understood as aesthetic appreciation, employing differ-ent sets of words. If one takes these distinct Hebrew words and assumes that all of the words may reside in a larger category such as beauty or aes-thetics, then one also lays down a heavy interpretive grid that forces many disparate concepts into the same anachronistic categorical space.

These words describe divine beauty (the first category): "On that day the branch of the Lord shall be beautiful [לצבי] and glorious [ולכבוד], and the fruit of the land shall be the pride and glory of the survivors of Israel" (Isa 4:2). I will call this "the beauty of majesty." Some words are used mostly to describe human beauty (the second category): "When he was about to enter Egypt, he [Abram] said to his wife Sarai, 'I know well that you are a woman beautiful in appearance'" (אשה יפת-מראה) (Gen 12:11). יפה is the word most commonly used for human beauty (Ringgren 1990, 218). It never describes God (Ferreter 2004, 124; Hubbard 1997, 58). I will call this "ordinary physical beauty."

> In the case of divine beauty the neighboring or supporting concepts are drawn from elsewhere: from the language of power (the biblical term "glory" suggests power as well as beauty, and goes along with terms like "majesty", "splendor", and "strength"), from that of ethics (most people think of Christ's beauty in terms of his moral and spiritual qualities) or from the more general divine attributes of holiness, perfection, goodness and excellence. (Sherry 2002, 54)

> Most of the texts in the Hebrew Bible ascribing beauty, splendor, and so on to God are from the Psalms, many of which are songs of praise, even love-poems, to God. (170)

There is no one word in Hebrew that comes close enough to the English word "beauty." Rather, there is a whole cluster of words that share some of beauty's meaning, but also include elements that would be completely alien to the English translation of "beauty," or in some cases they would excessively narrow the definition. So יפה (probably beauty's closest corresponding term) is not used even metaphorically for God or for the beauty of the cult.

In Yahweh's second speech to Job, in which he challenges Job to a duel, he uses many of these divine "beauty" words: "Deck yourself with majesty and dignity [he says]; clothe yourself with glory and splendor" (עדה נא גאון וגבה והוד והדר תלבש) (Job 40:10). In other words, Yahweh says, "You can only challenge me if you have divine qualities. But lacking those, you have no right to speak." These words (majesty, dignity, glory, splendor, and a few others) are most frequently used to describe God; less frequently, but still significantly, they refer to the majesty of the king or of the sacred places. They are words of authority. They are binding words that require prostration and obeisance. In the Hebrew Bible, they are seldom used to describe human physical beauty. William Dyrness (1985, 426) observes regarding the word commonly translated "splendor," "but of all the words for beauty, this one [הדר] seems best suited to God himself and seems appropriate in people only when they reflect (visibly) something of his character."

I am compelled to ask a foundational question, however: What makes these words (glory, honor, majesty, and splendor) beauty words? One may effectively argue that they are not beauty words at all. They have nothing to do with beauty, either with the Hebrew words I have called "ordinary physical beauty" or with beauty as understood in most contemporary discourse. I can conceive of only two reasons why these words might be regarded as beauty words. First, because (one might argue) *attraction* takes place. These words describe qualities that make God attractive. They draw people to God. But do they? More frequently they terrify. People who see the glory of God fear for their lives. In the Hebrew Bible, attraction has little to do with divine glory. Second, a long tradition exists of tying aesthetics in with the beauty of God. Might not that tradition exert backwards influence and compel us to think of God and beauty together in the Hebrew Bible? In any case, I have just a little more to say about "the beauty of majesty," and then I will leave it completely and focus on "ordinary physical beauty."

In English and related languages, beauty is an anthropocentric term, so words of beauty are attributed to God by analogy to human beauty.

Clearly, this does not occur in the Hebrew Bible. The concept of Yahweh's "beauty," "the beauty of holiness" (בהדרת-קדש, Ps 29:2), inhabits a different semantic world than the notions of human physical beauty. There is no one biblical aesthetic but rather (at least) two different aesthetics.

The Western intellectual tradition observes beauty in hierarchical terms, where God's perfect beauty is on the top, and every other thing in the universe is beautiful or not, depending upon how much or how little they resemble or reflect God's beauty. By the Hellenistic period, Jewish writers thought this way too. For example, in the Wisdom of Solomon, the author declares God "the author of beauty" (13:3). This might imply God as a source and pattern for all beauty and is the earliest place where it is at least possible to interpret it this way.

The Hebrew term יפה does not refer to God but is rather a unisex adjective that refers to both men and women (Hubbard 1997, 58). The word יפה is used to describe David and Absalom as well as Rachel, Abigail, Tamar (Absalom's daughter), Abishag, and others. We look in vain to find anything feminizing or demeaning in the word when it refers to men. To feminize a man would demean him in any patriarchal culture. In fact, when David does want to demean his rival Jonathan, he uses a different word entirely in his funeral oration:

> Saul and Jonathan, beloved and *lovely*!
> In life and in death they were not divided;
> they were swifter than eagles,
> they were stronger than lions. (2 Sam 1:23)[2]

David describes Jonathan's loveliness using the word נעם, which means "pleasant" or "pretty." David sought to diminish the stature of Jonathan by means of this speech, by feminizing him so as to strengthen his (David's) lock on the throne.

In this first section of the paper I focused on the eyes as a sign of beauty, but I also used this section to introduce notions of beauty and how they might have functioned in the Hebrew Bible. David's beautiful eyes manifest his power over other people. Leah's weak eyes signify her powerlessness, even though she is the more fertile wife. The beautiful one is regarded as the most powerful in a hierarchy. Very important in understanding beauty in the Hebrew Bible is the attraction, the energy that

---

2. See my discussion of David demeaning Jonathan in Penchansky 2001.

draws (what we might call) the beautiful object, and the one who perceives and experiences the beauty. That attraction has an effect on both parties in the transaction.

2. "I Am Black and Beautiful, O Daughters of Jerusalem, Like the Tents of Kedar, Like the Curtains of Solomon." (Song 1:5)

In the same verse (1 Sam 16:12) where the narrator introduces David's beautiful eyes, David's "ruddy" (אדמוני) complexion draws our attention. The color and condition of one's skin appears to be vitally important in understanding the claims of human physical beauty in the Hebrew Bible. David is beautiful, and his skin is ruddy (Hubbard 1997, 60). I assume that the word's relationship with "red" suggests that David's skin was burnt by the sun to a red color. However, Hend, my Arabic wife, explained to me, "Bedouins do not get red from the sun. They get dark." "What do you think it means?" I ask. "Ruddy is sensual. It makes me think of red meat and wine." I remain unconvinced that David's ruddiness bespeaks of his sensuality, but what Hend said makes my connections even more tenuous than they might have been. Does David's redness have symbolic significance, as Esau's hairy redness did, or does it have nothing to do with the color at all? I regard David's ruddiness as an indication of his status in that society, because it explains so many elements of the story and gets to the very heart of its tensions. We do not know whether to regard David's ruddiness as a beautiful trait or a detriment to his beauty. We hardly know what ruddiness might mean in this passage.

One must question whether David's beauty is at least partially because of his ruddiness or in spite of it. Do his beautiful eyes work together with his ruddiness to create a pleasing visual effect, or do the eyes cancel out the negative impact of his ruddy complexion? One interpretation notes that the elite, the leisure class, need not work outside. Their skin is "fair," because they have not experienced significant or regular exposure to the sun. Therefore, David's beauty would be in spite of his lower-class complexion. It should surprise no one that the ruddy ones tend to be the poor and rural.

The account of David's anointing by Samuel (1 Sam 16:13) hinges upon David's physical appearance, and the text in its present form says two exactly opposite things about that appearance. It says that David is beautiful and therefore worthy to assume power as king and receive admiration from the people. But Samuel is instructed not to pick according to outward appearance, and thus he picks David. "Do not look on his appearance or on the height of his stature, because I have rejected him; for the LORD does not see as mortals see; they look on the outward appearance, but the LORD looks on the heart" (1 Sam 16:7). So, presumably, David's brothers were more handsome (or beautiful) than David was, and Samuel was instructed to ignore their manly charms in favor of the younger and less-impressive David. David was in the field and therefore "ruddy," sun-burnt like a slave or a servant, the runt of the family. In English the word "fair" (light-skinned) becomes synonymous with beauty. Inexplicably, some translations of the Song of Songs render יפה as "fair" instead of "beautiful" at least some of the time. Darkness indicates class divisions—a poorer person, a peasant, a person of the land would be darker by virtue of being out in the sun. An upper-class person would be lighter, because of time spent indoors. Therefore, light skin is regarded as a sign of beauty.

So the text portrays David as beautiful and as nothing special at the same time. The text is ambiguous about the utility of David's physical appearance. This contrasts markedly with how everyone, including Samuel, had been impressed by Saul's very tall stature. The narrator observed that Kish had a son whose name was Saul, a handsome young man (בחור וטוב). There was not a man among the people of Israel more handsome than he (טוב ממנו); he stood head and shoulders above everyone else (1 Sam 9:2).

Here height is juxtaposed with being handsome. Generally, in the Bible, there are five features juxtaposed with "beautiful" or "handsome": eyes, skin, hair, flawlessness, and height. The first three serve as the organizing principle for my paper. One might also add "youth" as a characteristic of beauty. All the people described as beautiful were young. When Saul appeared before the people, Samuel could barely contain his own enthusiasm:

> When he took his stand among the people, he was head and shoulders taller than any of them. Samuel said to all the people, "Do you see the one whom the LORD has chosen? There is no one like him among all the people." (1 Sam 10:24)

There is ambiguity in the Deuteronomist's consideration of David's physical charms. On the one hand, his physical beauty demonstrates the worthiness of his choice (as with Saul), but, on the other hand, David is chosen because God looks on the heart. In terms of physical attractiveness, David is nothing special. He is ratty and feral. One might be tempted to say that David's beauty was inward, related to his character. In the Hebrew Bible, however, there is no notion of "inner beauty" until much later. Even though the sages praised the inner qualities of character as superior to physical beauty, they never suggested that these inner qualities were a superior kind of beauty: "Charm is deceitful, and beauty is vain, but a woman who fears the LORD is to be praised" (Prov 31:30).

In another example of the relationship of skin to perceptions of beauty, the unnamed lover in the Song of Songs introduces herself at the beginning of a series of poems, "I am black and beautiful, O daughters of Jerusalem, like the tents of Kedar, like the curtains of Solomon" (שחורה אני ונאוה בנות ירושלם כאהלי קדר כיריעות שלמה) (Song 1:5). Although the word describing the skin is different, "black" instead of "ruddy," both words suggest a reference to poor people who work in the sun. The next verse makes that clear. The woman declares: "Do not gaze at me because I am dark, because the sun has gazed on me" (1:6). The word "dark" (שחרחרת) is a variation on שחורה (black) and is clearly ascribed to the impact of the sun. So once again the question is, does her blackness make her comely, or is she so beautiful that the blackness makes no difference? Landy (1980, 63) notes this ambiguity: "The conjunction we in 'I am black and comely' may also mean but. She may be a dark beauty or a beauty in spite of her darkness. Her embarrassment is caused by her darkness, but is this enviable or contemptible, ugly or beautiful?"

One would presume that the poet compares the woman's blackness to tents and curtains, opulent and beautiful. It is unlikely that these two fabrics are chosen because they are despised. Solomon's curtains must be luxurious and well-appointed. I assume the same about Kedar's black tents—in Hebrew, Kedar means "black." Therefore, this serves as a strong argument that the blackness of the woman is regarded as a positive feature.

If David in 1 Samuel and the lover in Song of Songs are sun-burnt and poor, then they are beautiful in spite of their darker skin. However, if we read the text "black and beautiful," in what way might the skin's darkness be a sign of beauty? Traces of a pastoral attitude crop up from time to time in the ancient texts. It regards the "country people" as beautiful. They live a purer and less-corrupted lifestyle. They are noble. So, for the unnamed woman in Song of Songs and for the young David, their very sun-darkened appearance might have constituted a part of their appeal. Some have regarded the woman's blackness as an ethnic sign, an indication of her North African origin. I find this unlikely for reasons stated above.

David's subsequent career supports the idea that part of David's popularity was his rural and thus ruddy pedigree. People saw him (in spite of his imperious ways) as a down-to-earth leader, a man of the people. Queen Michal castigated him for this when he danced naked before the handmaids of his servants. But David knew that his uncouth behavior—in congruence with his darkened complexion—would appeal to the populace. "I will make myself yet more contemptible than this, and I will be abased in my own eyes; but by the maids of whom you have spoken, by them I shall be held in honor" (2 Sam 6:22). There are Arabic words to describe what might be called classical beauty, which is very much graded according to the lightness of the skin color, corresponding to the English word "fair." But there is also an Arabic word (masculine *asmar* and feminine *samra'a*) that indicates dark beauty. These words are used only for skin. It connects them with the earth and sweat, and they are words of very strong attraction.

The beloved is beautiful (יפה) either in spite of her darkness (שחורה) or because of it. From a pastoral perspective, darkness bespeaks the beauty of the earth, and the beautiful sun-darkened woman suggests a greater fertility, more full of the life force. Here fertility is a sign of the life force and thus a sign of beauty. In the Leah-Rachel story, fertility is pitted against beauty, and beauty wins.

3. "Your Hair Is Like a Flock of Goats, Moving Down the Slopes of Gilead." (Song 4:1)

In 2 Samuel, Absalom's hair underscores his beauty:

> In all Israel there was no one more praised for his beauty than Absalom; from the sole of his foot to the crown of his head, he could not be faulted. When he cut his hair—he shaved it once a year because his hair got too heavy—he would weigh the hair: two hundred shekels, king's weight.[3] (2 Sam 14:25–27, NJB)

Absalom's beauty is emphasized just before the mention of his hair (Hubbard 1997, 61). The hair becomes evidence of Absalom's beauty, implied by the juxtaposition. Like his father, Absalom is charming, persuasive, and charismatic. That is, he uses his beauty as a means to persuade people, to

---

3. There is an Arabic custom of fairly recent vintage where a baby's hair (after a certain age) would be cut, weighed, and that weight in gold distributed to the poor. Perhaps the author alludes to a similar practice here.

gain followers and admirers, to gain power. Hair, for Absalom, serves as a sign of power as well as beauty.

Absalom's beauty is also expressed in the flawlessness of his physical appearance. "Now in all Israel there was no one to be praised so much for his beauty as Absalom; from the sole of his foot to the crown of his head there was no blemish in him" (2 Sam 14:25). Although less-pronounced than the other features of attraction (eyes, hair, and skin), many different passages insist that a beautiful person has no flaws, handicaps, or disfigurements. In Daniel, the Babylonian officials choose youths who are good-looking. The description of them juxtaposes "handsome" and "without physical defect" to indicate that they are linked: "young men without physical defect and handsome [וטובי מראה], versed in every branch of wisdom, endowed with knowledge and insight, and competent to serve in the king's palace; they were to be taught the literature and language of the Chaldeans" (Dan 1:4). In the Song of Songs, beauty and flawlessness is again linked: "You are altogether beautiful, my love; there is no flaw in you" (Song 4:7). Absalom died when "his head caught fast in the oak and he was left hanging between heaven and earth, while the mule he was riding went on" (2 Sam 18:9, NJB). Although hair is not mentioned, it seems an obvious inference that his hair became tangled in the trees, which exposed him to murder (McCarter 1984, 406). There is nothing in the biblical text that suggests that Absalom hung by his hair, tangled in the branches of an overhanging tree. However, that tradition, I suspect, is very old. The emphasis on hair at the beginning might suggest the significance of hair at the end as well. This served as a cautionary tale against the deceptiveness of beauty for the ancient reader.

The account of Elisha and the forty-two children suggests another angle in the relationship of hair and beauty. Elisha encounters a group of children outside of Bethel, and they mock him: "Go away, baldhead! Go away" (2 Kgs 2:23). Their speech implies that baldness is a sign of shame.[4] The prophet punishes them by cursing them in Yahweh's name, thus calling down murderous bears to kill them. These children had implied that he was ugly, funny-looking, with a sexual deficiency. The connection of hair and sexuality occurs in some form in every culture of which I am aware. For example, sexuality and power are explicitly connected with hair in the Samson story. I also note the extreme reaction of Elisha and of

---

4. See my discussion of this passage in Penchansky 1999.

Yahweh, which suggests that something deeply personal and serious was at issue. Then I connect the dots. Hair equals potency and power. Cutting off hair equals loss of potency and power. Elisha's lack of hair suggests a lack of potency and power. The children make fun of him because of his baldness. Therefore, I conclude that they draw attention to his lack of potency. For men in the Hebrew Bible and beyond, hair serves as a sign of fertility and potency.

Hair is also linked to male potency, attractiveness, and beauty in the book of Numbers, where the Israelites establish a system by which non-priests may dedicate themselves to Yahweh for a period of time. In this Nazirite vow, one of the signs of the vow mentions hair: "As long as he is bound by his vow, no razor will touch his head until the time for which he has vowed himself to Yahweh is completed, he remains consecrated and will let his hair grow freely" (Num 6:5, NJB). There is much debate regarding the significance of the prohibition against the Nazirite cutting his hair. In Deuteronomy, the writer describes Joseph as a *nazir* and makes special reference to his hair: "May the hair grow thick on the head of Joseph, on the brow of the consecrated one (*nazir*) among his brothers" (Deut 33:16, NJB).

Within the Samson story, hair serves as a symbol of his strength. "A razor has never touched my head, because I have been God's Nazirite from my mother's womb. If my head were shorn, then my power would leave me and I should lose my strength and become like any other man" (Judg 16:17, NJB). What, then, is the meaning of hair in the Samson story? On one level, hair in this story is not a sign of beauty but rather a symbol of the vow and explicitly a sign of his strength. However, the symbolism goes deeper than that. There is a notable sexual element to the story, and strength here also refers to sexual potency. When Samson lost his hair, it was a castration, and as a result Samson became passive and docile. Absalom's haircut was decidedly not a castration. It represented his largess and the overflow of his beauty and power. Every year the hair was too heavy for him. As in the Elisha story, hair serves as a substitute for the penis, and the cutting of Samson's hair was a kind of castration. Connected with that, the insult to Elisha was serious, because the children's accusation hinted at the prophet's sexual inadequacy.

Women's hair is very different. In Isaiah, the prophet condemns the beautiful women of his homeland, threatening them with poverty and enslavement: "Then, instead of perfume, a stink; instead of belt, a rope, instead of hair elaborately dressed, a shaven scalp, instead of gorgeous clothes, sacking round the waist, and brand marks instead of beauty" (Isa 3:24, NJB). The elements of beauty are stripped away. They include "hair elaborately dressed," in this case a sign of feminine beauty and wealth, now shaven and violated (Ferretter 2004, 129–30). Hair serves as a sign of privilege, along with the other elements (perfume, belt, clothing). A shaven scalp signifies humiliation, defeat, and degradation. The issue of hair and its relationship with beauty comes up in a later story. Susanna was very graceful and beautiful to look at (Sus 1:2), and her hair was covered to protect her modesty. I assume here that the covering was something like the modern-day *hijab* and that its intention was to cover the hair, not the face, neck, or shoulders. But evil men wanted access. "She was veiled, so the wretches made her unveil in order to feast their eyes on her beauty" (Sus 1:32, NJB). The level of abuse and excess gets worse: "The two elders stood up, with all the people round them, and laid their hands on her head" (Sus 1: 34, NJB).

Susanna was a modest woman who showed her modesty by concealing her beauty. Her beauty was embodied in her hair, which she therefore covered. First, the elders exposed her hair for all to see. Then they touched her head in order to gain access to her beauty and to sexually humiliate her.

In the New Testament, a "sinful woman" wipes Jesus' feet with her hair. "She waited behind him at his feet, weeping, and her tears fell on his feet, and she wiped them away with her hair; then she covered his feet with kisses and anointed them with the ointment" (Luke 7:38, NJB). Hair, which is "the glory of the woman," she uses for a menial task:

> Decide for yourselves; does it seem fitting that a woman should pray to God without a veil? Does not nature itself teach you that if a man has long hair, it is a disgrace to him, but when a woman has long hair, it is her glory? After all, her hair was given to her to be a covering. (1 Cor 11:14–15, NJB) (see Schüssler Fiorenza 1983, 226–35)

For a woman, long hair is her "glory." Paul has combined in this passage the two realms of beauty found separate in earlier Hebrew texts. Glory (δοξα) is a word in the "beauty of majesty" category. Here it equals a woman's beauty. Long hair is a woman's beauty, but/and/so it must be concealed. Paul confuses us as to whether the hair is a covering or whether the hair should be covered. Contrary to the Hebrew Bible, where Absalom's long hair was a sign of his beauty, the apostle believes that beautiful long hair is not appropriate for a man.

For Paul, the iconography of hair has clearly changed from the time of the Absalom story, so what was considered beautiful and attractive in a man has come to be regarded as disgraceful in Paul's eyes. First, Paul has shifted the notion of beauty, which in the Hebrew Bible was genderless, and now "beauty" has become a female trait. To manifest long hair as a sign of beauty would be shameful for a male person. Second, Paul reflects the hierarchy of beauty one finds in later theological thought, that God's perfect beauty is the pattern and measure of all other manifestations of beauty in the world. He would not call a woman's hair "her glory" unless he believed that her beauty (as represented by her hair) manifested something of God's glory.

With men, cutting hair reflected the loss of strength and was a form of castration. Touching a woman's hair sexually humiliated her. The extreme reaction of Elisha to the children's insult indicates how his heart was cut by their words. Finally, Paul's reverse statement about the shame of a man's (long) hair and his appeal to nature suggests that Paul's argument was made against the conventional wisdom of his time. I make the following connections. Hair equals beauty. Male hair equals male potency. Loss of male hair equals ugliness, revulsion, shame, and castration. For the woman, too, hair equals beauty. That beauty must be covered, so that men will be able to control their urges in her presence. If the woman strays, strange men will uncover her hair in public and rudely handle it. Absalom, long before Paul changed its meaning, could flaunt his sexuality in an open and free manner. In the Hebrew Bible and the New Testament, a woman must always remain covered. She must conceal her sexuality by covering her hair.

4. Beauty in a Larger Context: Aesthetics, Theology, and the Hebrew Bible

"In the beauty of the lilies, Christ was born across the sea with a glory in his bosom that transfigures you and me" ("Battle Hymn of the Republic"). Von Rad wrote about the subject of aesthetics in his *Old Testament Theology*. He concluded that (1) Israel had no capacity for abstract thought concerning beauty. He said, "Beauty can hardly be made the object of separate study in the OT without distorting the material" (von Rad 1962, 365, 430). (2) Israel contributed little in the production of beauty (art), because they were proscribed by the second commandment; and (3) the only beauty the Israelites excelled in was poetry and narrative. He concluded that they were precritical, naïve, and yet more verbal. He was wrong on all counts. The only reason he thought they could not abstract is because his abstraction was different.

Roman Catholic systematic theologians have focused on biblical aesthetics. Hans Urs von Balthasar dedicated seven of his massive sixteen-volume systematic theology to *The Glory of the Lord*, which he identified as a theological aesthetic. He dedicated two of those volumes to Scripture, one to the Old Testament, and one to the New. But von Balthasar, and the writers who followed him, only look upon human beauty as a reflection of the beauty of God (Sherry 2002, 2). They anachronistically ignore the different way that the Israelites organized their understanding of beauty.

Likewise, certain evangelical Protestant theologians have written on the topic of beauty in the Bible. What is it about biblical aesthetics that so attracted them? These evangelicals seek to isolate a single unified biblical aesthetic, which reflects their larger quest for a single unifying and non-contradictory system to encompass all of the biblical revelation. There is no single aesthetic, nor can there be.

The Marxists write about aesthetics, but for the most part they are concerned with the political role that art plays in industrialized societies. They define art in terms of the means of production and remain suspicious of any claims for art being nonpolitical. Their concern for contemporary art makes their writings of limited utility to this project.

So I return to the two irreducible ideas regarding beauty found in the Hebrew Bible: attraction and power. Beauty is the immediate, visceral response that a person has to the attractiveness of another. The experience of beauty is not a judgment of the intellect. But, on the other hand (the second irreducible idea), beauty signifies power: the more beautiful, the more powerful—and the ones who decide who and what is beautiful have the most power of all.

Most have recognized that the perception of beauty is an immediate experience with a strong biological and intuitive component. It is not cognitive or reflective. There is a second point in the aesthetic process where one interrogates the experience, the perception of beauty. We can interpret it theologically (beauty as a reflection of God's glory), biologically or evolutionarily (the response is hardwired to the brain so as to advance the species), or using Freudian, Jungian, or Marxist grids. Each of these asks and seeks to answer the questions: What is beauty? What are the criteria? Who decides?

5. Conclusion

There is ambiguity in the depiction of beautiful David and beautiful Rachel. In the David story, God does not look at the outward (where beauty resides), and later, although David's charm/charisma/beauty got him everything he wanted, it destroyed him. Likewise, in the Rachel story, might Leah not stand for those who excelled in all that society valued in women, except for the one thing that apparently counted more than all the others, physical beauty? Leah did everything right, followed all the rules, bargained for the love potions, and traded for privileges to her husband's night chambers, but she never gained her husband's affections or the proper status in the household, a status she should have held by virtue of being older, the first married, the only one with children, and the first one to give her husband male heirs.

If the narrator wanted the reader to sympathize with Rachel's beauty, why introduce Leah? How can our sympathies for Leah fail to dampen our joy for Rachel at the birth of her first son?

The beautiful one—declared so by the narrator or by another character—has privileges over the nonbeautiful. However, I remain suspicious of the privileges afforded to the beautiful. In the Leah-Rachel story and the David narration, the authors timidly and tentatively call into question the justice that confers privileges upon the good-looking. But even if they had not raised these questions, it still behooves us to question the determination and the power of beauty in the Bible and to question the very category itself.

On the other hand, to ascribe something as beautiful works on a noncognitive, nonrational level. As such, it gets to deep and often unconscious ideological commitments on the part of the author/poet/narrator and the society that she or he represents. Does ordinary physical beauty in the Bible always disappoint? The Israelites hoped in the promise of David's beautiful eyes, only to be seduced by a murderous despot. The reader hoped that Rachel's beauty and grace portended success and happiness in her life, but a life of conflict and disappointment ended in the blood pooling under the birth stool. That is why the sages decried beauty as vain and recommended faithfulness and piety over looks.

But the experience of beauty creates a liminal moment—this moment contains great promise, great creativity, but also great danger. It threatens the boundaries of our identity. However, in spite of our suspicions, beauty remains a primal force. To shut ourselves out from the experience of beauty condemns one to aridity.

Works Cited

Dyrness, William A. 1985. Aesthetics in the Old Testament: Beauty in Context. *JETS* 28:421–32.

Eagleton, Terry. 1990. *The Ideology of the Aesthetic*. Oxford: Blackwell.

Ferretter, Luke. 2004. The Power and the Glory: The Aesthetics of the Hebrew Bible. *Literature and Theology* 18:123–38.

Hubbard, Robert L. 1997. The Eyes Have It: Theological Reflections on Human Beauty. *ExAud* 13:57–72.

Landy, Francis. 1980. Beauty and the Enigma: An Inquiry into Some Interrelated Episodes of the Song of Songs. *JSOT* 17:55–106.

McCarter, P. Kyle. 1984. *II Samuel*. AB 9. Garden City, N.Y.: Doubleday.

Penchansky, David. 1999. *What Rough Beast: Images of God in the Hebrew Bible*. Louisville: Westminster.

———. 2010. Four Vignettes from the Life of David: Recollections of the Royal Court. Pages 55–65 in *The Fate of King David: the Past and Present of a Biblical Icon*. Edited by Tod Linafelt, Claudia V. Camp, and Timothy K. Beal. New York: T&T Clark.

Rad, Gerhard von. 1962. *Old Testament Theology*. Vol. 1. Translated by D. M. G. Stalker. New York: Harper & Row, 1962.

Ringgren, Helmer. 1990. יפה. Pages 218–20 in vol. 6 of *Theological Dictionary of the Old Testament*. Edited by G. Johannes Botterweck and Helmer Ringgren. Translated by David E. Green. 15 vols. Grand Rapids: Eerdmans.

Schüssler Fiorenza, Elisabeth. 1983. *In Memory of Her: A Feminist Theological Reconstruction of Christian Origins*. New York: Crossroad.

Sherry, Patrick. 2002. *Spirit and Beauty: An Introduction to Theological Aesthetics*. 2nd ed. London: SCM.

Viladesau, Richard. 1999. *Theological Aesthetics: God in Imagination, Beauty and Art*. New York: Oxford University Press.

Wilde, Oscar. 1891. "The Decay of Lying: An Observation." Pages 3–57 in *Intentions and the Soul of Man*. London: Methuen.

Yachin and Boaz in Jerusalem and Rome

Richard J. Bautch

How is it that two columns curiously described in 1 Kings and 2 Chronicles capture the imagination of Renaissance artists and find expression in their tapestries and monuments? This paper takes up the *Nachleben* of Yachin and Boaz, the preeminent columns in Solomon's Temple, and examines why these ancient architectural fixtures appealed to a later aesthetic sensibility. Jean Fouquet, Raphael and his school, and Gian Lorenzo Bernini, among others, depicted or in some instances actually created columns that were modeled on those of Solomon's Temple but with an added feature, a partial fluting that resulted in spiral columns. The construction of the new St. Peter's Basilica in the sixteenth and seventeenth centuries, in fact, provided multiple occasions for the columns and other features of Solomon's Temple to be rearticulated in Christian architecture. The argument here is that what made the Solomonic columns especially attractive to select artists of the Renaissance period is the fact that the two pillars reflected aesthetic and political dimensions of the society that created them. The later artists, along with their patrons, sought no less to fashion in their own realm expressions of beauty that were consistent with the sociopolitical realities of their day.

1. Yachin and Boaz in 1 Kings and 2 Chronicles

To appreciate how the two Solomonic columns function in a later historical context, their original relationships to aesthetics and politics in ancient Israel will be elucidated. It is, of course, anachronistic to speak of aesthetics in ancient Israel, but quite clearly the biblical writers incorporated into their texts different senses of beauty, especially human beauty (see Gen 29:16–17; 1 Sam 16:12). The yoking of beauty and politics is attested in the Hebrew Bible and was, as David Penchansky observes, evident in the

earliest aesthetic debates (in this volume, see 49). The physical presence
of two columns just outside the Solomonic temple gave rise to just such
an interplay of politics and aesthetics. It is within the description of Solomon's Temple—at 1 Kgs 7:13–22, 41–42; 2 Chr 3:15–17—that the two columns referred to as Yachin and Boaz are distinguished by their construction in bronze (נחשת), their elaborate decoration, and their immense size
(Busink 1970, 299–321). The columns are presented as 18 cubits high, each
topped with a florid capital of 5 cubits.[1] Despite their great height, they
do not reach up to the temple's roof, nor do they support the structure
otherwise. Because the columns are freestanding, their value would seem
to be largely symbolic. That is to say, a few scholars understand the twin
columns to be decorative or ornamental, but most ascribe to the structures
a symbolic significance (Wright 1941, 17–31).

The symbolism bespeaks political exigencies that confronted Solomon: consolidating his father's territorial gains and establishing secure
borders.[2] To these two challenges, a third was added: building a temple
to the God of Israel. Yachin and Boaz played a role in meeting all three
objectives, but to understand how this occurred one must step back and
consider how religious structures functioned within the societies of the
ancient Near East.

Twin columns are attested at various Iron Age temples in the Levant,
including ʿAin Dara in northern Syria (Monson 2000, 20–35), which provides a close parallel to the columns of Solomon's Temple and other features as well. Samuel Yeivin was one of the first to consider the significance
of columns that were part of a religious edifice in the ancient world. His
article "Yachin and Boaz" has been cited frequently in the fifty years since
its publication (Yeivin 1959, 6–22). By adducing parallels with the nomadic

---

1. The Chronicler reports a greater height of 35 cubits for each column (2 Chr
3:15). Commentators hold that this figure is simply the sum total of all the given
measurements in the Chronicler's source, 1 Kgs 7:15–16, where each column is 18
cubits high, with a circumference of 12 cubits, and a capital that is 5 cubits high
(Japhet 1993, 557).

2. Although the books of Kings likely originated in the court of Josiah, with subsequent editing in the exile, the scribes responsible for the text worked from source
material, namely, records of the Judean royal court dating back to Solomon's reign in
the tenth century B.C.E. On these grounds, I approach Yachin and Boaz as effects of
Solomon's rule, although it would be legitimate and worthwhile to analyze the columns in light of the social conditions during Josiah's reign or the exilic period (Long
1984, 32).

tribes of pre-Islamic Arabia, Yeivin showed that, in Israelite life, religion and ritual were not compartmentalized or isolated. He rightly concluded that the two bronze columns in front of the Jerusalem temple symbolized the permanent abiding of Yahweh therein. This view has been developed from an archaeological perspective by Carol Meyers (1983, 173), who has shown that the exact location of the columns (באולם; 1 Kgs 7:19) should be understood as a courtyard, with the two pillars marking the entrance to this space as they would signal the portal to God's house; that is, "providing the visual link to the unseen grandeur within, ... the columns represented to the world at large that which existed unseen within the building."

Implicit in the conclusions of Yeivin and Meyers is the view that the cultic structures of ancient Israel are to be seen as part of the political ideology of the realm. In the time when Solomon built the temple, the nascent Davidic monarchy aimed to consolidate its territorial gains and secure its borders within the region. Its method was straightforward: enhance the king's prestige by associating the ruler with the national deity and its might, then display the divine might through a temple structure (Scott 1939, 143–49).

The monikers Yachin and Boaz (1 Kgs 7:21) reinforce such an ideology. Yachin, from the root כון ("he establishes"), could be indicative of an expression such as "he (God) will establish the throne of David and his kingdom to his seed forever."[3] Boaz, conversely, could be rendered "in his strength," if בעז is pointed with a *shewa* and a *holem*.[4] Thus, the full expression would refer to the strength of either the king or of God; if the latter is the case, the king would be associated with the deity's might, as in the Davidic Ps 21 (21:1). Such analysis of the Hebrew roots כון and בעז recalls that monuments could be used to associate royal authority with a deity. In her analysis of Solomon's Temple, Meyers (1983, 175) reports that in the ancient Near East the "essentially coercive power" represented by dynastic states derived its legitimacy from the close connection of such states with divine sovereignty.

At the same time, Yachin and Boaz serve an aesthetic purpose, as they exemplify "the beauty of majesty," a notion that is found in Penchansky's research on biblical aesthetics and authority. Penchansky distinguishes

---

3. See Davidic passages with the root כון, such as 2 Sam 7:12, 13, 16, 26; Isa 9:6; 16:5; Ps 89:4–5, 22, 37–38.

4. MT's pointing of a *ḥōlem* and a *pataḥ* is difficult, as it renders the expression "fleet," which is not easily associated with a column.

the beauty of majesty from human physical beauty (52). The two, in fact, are incomparable, because the beauty of majesty refers to divine qualities or divine effects that are sensorially pleasing. Penchansky's examples include Isa 4:2, which describes the branch of the Lord as beautiful (צבי) and glorious (כבוד). Through specialized vocabulary, the beauty of majesty is associated uniquely with God, although the fact that beauty is an anthropocentric term leads Penchansky to speculate that "words of beauty are attributed to God by analogy to human beauty" (52). He adds, "These words … are most frequently used to describe God; less frequently, but still significantly, they refer to the majesty of the king or of the sacred places" (53). The distinction between human and divine beauty is therefore not absolute, and Yachin and Boaz standing in the sacred space of the temple are evidence of this fact.

It would appear that Yachin and Boaz represent both human beauty as well as the beauty of majesty, if one follows the analysis of Meyers. Her claim is that certain structures outside the temple provide the visual link to the unseen grandeur within its walls. In this view, Yachin and Boaz reflect not simply the human hands that made them but also the deity whose majesty transcends human greatness. The very notion of the beauty of majesty implies that human beauty and divine beauty, albeit analogous, are incomparable. With the case of 1 Kgs 7, however, the issue is more complex. In the political matrix of David and Solomon, the connection between the deity and the two columns may be put in the service of more mundane concerns, namely, an earthly ruler's desire to consolidate power and in the process burnish his image. In other words, the columns can function as expressions of human traditions. The beauty of majesty refers to God's grandeur, but it can be arrogated by a king such as Solomon to enhance his majesty. The record from ancient Israel correlates aesthetic, theological, and political forces to render a complex portrait of Yachin and Boaz.[5]

2. Solomonic Reflexes in the Christian Tradition

This section of the paper briefly outlines a trajectory whereby elements of design associated with Solomon's Temple became current in Renaissance

---

5. The complexity in question arises whenever one develops a historical account of a work of art. Terry Eagleton (1990, 4) writes of "historical or ideological contextualizations of art" as if they were two distinct phenomena, but invariably it is the case that art is associated with the social practices and politics of the artist's time.

art. Since it is not the focus of this study, the treatment of Solomonic reflexes is suggestive, not exhaustive. Knowing the manner in which Solomonic columns came to the attention of artists centuries later is useful background for an analysis of the new St. Peter's Basilica and the adjacent Vatican palace, where Solomonic columns were used in the work of Bernini and Raphael, respectively.

It is a curious set of facts that, on the one hand, allegorical representations of Solomon's Temple were virtually absent from early Christian art (Ferber 1976, 24), and, on the other hand, by 1225 there stood in the cathedral of Würzburg two monumental columns with the names Iachim and Booz inscribed on their capitals (Cahn 1976, 51). What happened in the first Christian millennium leading to the rise of Solomonic art forms? It is revealing to consider both the legacy of Solomon and developments in the design of columns.

Walter Cahn reports that, in the middle of the ninth century, Western Christianity began to project the Solomonic legacy upon the Dome of the Rock and the Al-Aqsa Mosque, the Muslim sanctuaries that the Umayyads had built in the temple *temenos* (45). Certain Christians claimed that Solomon had built these structures, and this far-fetched notion gained traction in the eleventh century, when, as a result of the Crusades, the two structures in question were converted to houses of Christian worship. Alongside the Dome of the Rock and Al-Aqsa Mosque, there were added cloisters and a second church during the years 1099–1187, when Jerusalem was ruled by the Crusaders. In the twelfth century, the Christian West had an increased awareness of the structures on the Temple Mount in Jerusalem, and images of Solomon and the temple appeared with increasing frequency in Romanesque art. Curiously, the temple now included cloisters, a colonnaded space more extensive than that produced by Yachin and Boaz, the outstanding columns in the biblical account. An intrusion from the Crusader period, the cloisters became associated with the Solomonic legacy as it was being harmonized with Christian themes.

The cloisters are in fact a textbook example of artists conjoining Solomonic and Christian legends. Cahn (1976, 49–51) states that the "cloister" of Solomon became associated with the meeting place of the apostles when the Holy Spirit descended upon them (Acts 2:1–4), and into this blend was included another biblical reference, the seven columns of the house of wisdom (Prov 9:1). In some of the European cloisters built during this time, the apostles are portrayed as perched atop piers in the four corners. It is intriguing to think about the possible lines of influence between narratives generated in Jerusalem or more generally the Near East and art produced in the West. Yet Cahn discounts any East-to-West influence: "What we have here, then, is a Solomonic explanation or justification for an existing state of affairs, itself Solomonic in a much more remote or only symbolic sense" (50). That is to say, when the legacy of Solomon is manifest in Western art, the details are not based on historical accounts of the Jerusalem temple, and they reflect rather the projection of a Solomonic ethos upon architecture indigenous to Europe, such as the cloister.

Such is the case with the columns in the cathedral of Würzburg. The two columns date to this period (ca. 1225) and bear the names Iachim and Booz on their capitals. Although the columns now stand in front of the baptismal chapel off the south aisle of the cathedral, they were originally situated on the first part of the porch at the western entrance to the structure. Such a plan suggests that the columns were intended to function as did the historical Yachin and Boaz in pronouncing the presence of the deity within the structure. The plan for the Würzburg columns, however, can be traced back not to Jerusalem but in all likelihood to a prior bishop of Würzburg, Theodorich, who earlier in the thirteenth century wrote and circulated a description of the Holy Land. Through his authorial celebration of Jerusalem, which extended to descriptions of column paintings and mosaics, Theodorich conjured up the temple *mythos* that could be applied to the construction of his cathedral and thereby enhance the reputation of his see (Folda 1996, 90–91).

A similar situation pertains to a set of twelve serpentine columns that were incorporated into the first St. Peter's Basilica begun sometime during the first half of the fourth century. Winding sinuously, the columns appear to be of Greek origin, and they are said to have come as a gift from Constantine.[6] Originally the columns served to screen the altar of St. Peter, and with the rebuilding of the basilica in the sixteenth century ten of the columns were reused as supports for a temporary structure, a canopy or "ciborium" located in the back of the apse. At this point in time, during the Renaissance, the columns' Greek origins had been embellished with an additional layer of "history"; it was commonly believed that the twelve columns came from the temple of Solomon. William Kirwin (1997, 80) refers to this belief as the "well established legend of columns originally in Solo-

---

6. According to the *Liber Pontificalis*, six were given by Constantine, and the remaining were a present from the Byzantine exarch in the eighth century.

mon's portico transported to Rome after Christ's death." It is not certain when this notion of the columns' Solomonic origin first arose, but Cahn claims that "it was no earlier than 1350" (56). In fact, a date in the late fourteenth or even fifteenth century is most likely. The resurgent papacy returned from Avignon in 1377, and after a series of popes regained the Church's lands, Pope Nicholas V (r. 1447–1455) began to build ambitiously in the capital, Rome. The pope and his artists, such as Alberti, envisioned a Rome that evoked Jerusalem: "With the restored papacy's ultimate goal of Catholic domination of the united eastern and western Mediterranean, both real and imagined architecture from the Holy Land was co-opted into a vision of papal destiny; ancient legend and history were similarly reinterpreted to apply" (Tanner 2010, 14). By the end of the fifteenth century, Solomonic art forms were readily found in European churches. The twelve winding columns in St. Peter's are especially important, because in consolidating the Solomonic legacy and the columnar form, they prepare for the work of Bernini in this preeminent basilica and Raphael in the Sistine Chapel.

3. Apostrophes to Pope Leo X

Early in his pontificate, Pope Leo X (1513–1521) commissiond the artist Raphael to create tapestries for the palace chapel of Pope Sixtus IV, that is, the Sistine Chapel. Such enhancements of the Sistine Chapel had in fact been ongoing since 1506, when the foundation stone of the new St. Peter's Basilica was laid, and the subsequent destruction of the earlier building made it increasingly difficult to celebrate liturgies in its midst. At this point, many ceremonies were transferred to the Sistine Chapel, whose interior was beautified through the addition of frescoes by Michelangelo and other works of art.

A complement to the frescoes, the tapestries of Raphael depicted various scenes from the lives of Peter and Paul, including Peter's healing of a lame man at the Beautiful Gate of the Jerusalem temple (Acts 3:1–2). In establishing the scene, Raphael employed a distinctive type of column, the serpentine Solomonic columns long associated with the chancel in St. Peter's Basilica. Moreover, Raphael set two of the helical columns together in the foreground of his scene in a manner that evokes Yachin and Boaz as they are described in the Hebrew Bible. There were no doubt practical reasons why Raphael incorporated the Solomonic column; John Shearman (1972, 56) suggests that that the fluted columns' "familiar function as *cancello* in the basilica would clarify the situation depicted," namely, that a healing was taking place in a renown house of prayer, in this case, the ancient temple. Shearman further suggests, however, that Raphael was motivated by other concerns related to the Solomonic character of the Sistine Chapel and ultimately to the regal legacy being cultivated by his patron Leo X.

Especially after its rebuilding by Pope Sixtus IV near the end of the fifteenth century, the Sistine Chapel evoked myriad aspects of the Jerusalem temple (Shearman 1972, 8). The architecture as a whole was patterned on that of Solomon's Temple. The internal measurements were 40.9 meters (134 ft) long by 13.4 meters (44 ft) wide, roughly the dimensions of the temple of Solomon as given in the Hebrew Bible (in cubits). The seven candlesticks in the candelabra of Sixtus symbolized the seven gifts of the divine spirit that are enumerated in Isa 11:2. An eighth-century tradition associates seven lit candles with the seven gifts and relates them to the seven-branched candlestick, the menorah, in the temple of Solomon (Exod 25:31–40). It is plausible that Raphael sought to amplify these associations between the Jerusalem temple and the Sistine Chapel by creating for the latter a biblical scene featuring Solomonic columns. In Raphael's day, Shearman contends, "no one … seems to have doubted the legend that they [the columns] came from Solomon's temple" (1972, 56). The artist, however, likely knew the truth, according to Shearman. Specifically, through his studies Raphael knew that the Beautiful Gate would feature not columns but doors of Corinthian brass, and he further knew that the portal structure in question was built not by Solomon but by the postexilic community in Judah centuries later (57). The question becomes, why was Raphael complicit in a pious fraud?

The answer may have to do with the regal legacy being cultivated by his patron Leo X. It is worth recalling that in the political matrix of David and Solomon an earthly ruler could consolidate his power and in the process burnish his image by exploiting the presumed connection between the deity and the two columns Yachin and Boaz. That is to say, the columns could function as expressions of royal traditions and elevate the king in question to a level associated with a divine being. Although Leo did not seek his own apotheosis, upon his election as pope he was extolled in terms that were at once Solomonic, Davidic, and christological.

Shearman even writes of the "deliberately Messianic, even soteriological allegorizing of the election of Leo" (1972, 17). He adds that "there was little doubt that these apostrophes inspired in Leo the ambition to fulfill such high expectations, and that his policies were to some extent shaped by the pressures that they expressed." The expectations were evident from Leo's earliest days as pope. In a sermon delivered in April 1513, Simon Begnius, bishop of Modrusia, cited Zech 9:9 to imply a likeness between Leo and Jesus Christ. In the same sermon, Rev 5:5 was invoked with its reference to the lion of the tribe of Judah, the root of David, a prophecy thought to be fulfilled in the new pope. Begnius calls Leo "our Savior," and there were other such paeans to him.[7] One of the most interesting relates Leo to the lion of Judah who alone could loose the seven seals featured in the book of Revelation (17).[8]

While Begnius preached Leo's praises, Raphael honored his patron through his art. To connect Leo concretely to the legacy of Solomon and Christ, Raphael's temple scene incorporated the fluted columns and thus associated the pope with healing and peacemaking, which were two preeminent qualities of Solomon. Ancient traditions developed the notion of Solomon as a man of rest/peace largely on the basis of 1 Chr 22:9, while Solomon's curative powers and his authority over demons are highlighted by Josephus (*A.J.* 8.45–49, Thackeray). In light of such Solomonic legacies, there had been puns on the name of this Medici pope and *Christus medicus*, a title that could refer not only to Jesus but as well to his forerunner, Solomon the healer (Kreitzer 2005, 485). Raphael's tapestry was a further play on these puns. The pope was also referred to as the *rex pacificus*, another title shared by Solomon and Christ, the "prince of peace." In the words of Shearman (1972, 57), "the role of the Solomonic columns in the tapestry of Raphael, then, is likely symbolic, either of the miraculous healing powers associated with one of them or of Solomon himself, *rex pacificus*, or perhaps of both."

4. THE CANNONS AND THE COLUMNS

In the biblical account of 1 Kgs 7:13–14, a certain Hiram of Tyre is the skilled smith who creates the columns Yachin and Boaz out of bronze (נחשת).

---

7. This portion of Begnius's address to Leo is preserved in Jelf 1847, 521.

8. A more recent figure to assume this role was Vernon Howell, that is, David Koresh, leader of the ill-fated Branch Davidian compound in Waco, Texas. While sequestered in the compound with his followers, Howell claimed that he was in the process of opening the seven seals exegetically. Not surprisingly, many dismissed Howell as delusional. See Tabor and Gallagher 1995, 53–58.

Hiram's pedigree as well as his acumen with bronze are elaborated: "He was the son of a widow of the tribe of Naphtali, whose father, a man of Tyre, had been an artisan in bronze; he was full of skill, intelligence, and knowledge in working bronze. He came to King Solomon, and did all his work" (1 Kgs 7:14 NRSV). Hiram possesses skill (חכמה), intelligence (תבונה), and knowledge (דעת) as an artificer of bronze. When Hiram is introduced in 2 Chr 2:12, he is said to be "a man of wisdom who has [literally 'knows'] understanding." Although the Chronicler has clearly changed the syntax of his source, 1 Kgs 7:14, he retains the three qualities there attributed to Hiram: יודע בינה חכם. The fact that in all three cases the Chronicler uses a form of the word that is grammatically different from his source, along with the fact that in general the Chronicler's description of Hiram is more glowing, suggests that as the Chronicler's expression diverged from 1 Kgs 7, he nonetheless retained the three qualities attributed to Hiram as if they were essential to describing the craftsman's work.

Curiously, in the book of Proverbs these are three attributes of the God who created heaven, earth, and the seas as well. When the author of Proverbs remarks on God's חכמה, תבונה, and דעת, there is established a connection between the deity and the works of Hiram. Martin Mulder (1998, 305) observes, "Just as, on a macrocosmic scale, YHWH once founded the earth by his wisdom and by his understanding established the heavens and by his knowledge cleaved the deeps (Prov 3:19), so Hiram goes to work microcosmically to fashion the place [i.e., the temple] for YHWH." The point could not be simpler: to make great columns of bronze, as does Hiram, is to ally with the powers of God. This insight was not lost on Maffeo Barberini, who as Pope Urban VIII (1623–1644) chose Gian Lorenzo Bernini to be his Hiram of Tyre.

The papal installation of Leo X along with the subsequent efforts to link that pope to Solomon's legacy illustrated how, aesthetically, what Penchansky has identified as the majesty of beauty was operative in the Italian Renaissance. There was a blurring of the biblical distinction between divine beauty, as well as power, and the beauty that humans create. Similar dynamics emerged a century later with Urban VIII. To wit, in September 1623, Urban was "crowned" pope in a ceremony in St. Peter's Basilica. The coronation was dramatic in many respects, and it has led William Kirwin to comment: "Papal ceremony and liturgy had been since the fourth century two of the church's most compelling public actions, for they functioned as a collective reaffirmation of *the divine powers of majesty and faith that were invested in the office of the papacy*" (1997, 17, emphasis added).

That is to say, the ceremony and artistry that attend the papacy can corroborate the view that the pope's majesty is conjoined to that of God. When Urban was crowned and gave his blessing, the cannon at the Castle of the Holy Angel was fired, and the crowd began cheering the new pope.

The bronze cannon would become crucial both tactically and symbolically during the pontificate of Urban VIII, who was a spiritual leader as well as the commander in chief of the Papal States. At the outset, Urban indicated that he would improve the spiritual and temporal governance of the church in concrete ways.[9] Temporally, he sought to rearm his troops with stronger armor and state-of-the-art weaponry, such as new long and short arms and especially the bronze cannon. These efforts amounted to the refortification of the Papal States through the manufacture of bronze. The bronze cannon would be especially helpful for defending and securing the Vatican perimeter at points such as the Castle of the Holy Angel. Toward this end, Urban renovated the bronze foundry at the Vatican and increased its production to meet his military objectives. The retooling paid additional dividends, moreover, as it now became possible to conceive of and create a baldachin, a permanent bronze canopy to stand over the altar and tomb of the apostle Peter inside St. Peter's Basilica. For years artists had theorized about erecting such a structure, but the plan became feasible only with the increased production of bronze at the Vatican foundry. Kirwin thus describes the "technological implications" of Urban's project as twofold: "the conjunction of artistic ornaments and militaristic instruments" (7–8). Kirwin adds, "a close reading of the documents revealed to me that Urban's rearmament of the Vatican was the *sine qua non* for the successful manufacture of a suitable bronze cover" (7–8).

In fact, at the bronze foundry within the Vatican, the pillars of the baldachin were made alongside the long arms and cannons. From January 1626 to March 1627 the foundry produced eighty-four cannon pieces and the twenty columnar parts that make up the four spiral columns of

---

9. In 1623 the Papal States were not formidable, as they were about 400 kilometers long and 200 kilometers wide. Rather, the great states of the day were the Hapsburg dynasty and France. Urban pictured himself acting as the mediator of the great powers and in that sense becoming on a par with them. The conflict of the day was the Thirty Years War, which spiked in 1630 when the fortunes of the Protestant side improved dramatically (the war went on until 1648). Urban saw this war as a duel to the death in which the forces of the Holy Spirit would prevail (Kirwin 1997, 7–8).

the baldachin (each column comprises five pieces). By late May 1627, the columns had been assembled and set upon pedestals at the four corners of the altar above the sepulcher of Peter. The columns came into place rapidly through an eighteen-month production process; it would be another six years until the canopy was added to complete the baldachin. Again, Kirwin's commentary is illuminating: "The manufacture of the cannon and the columns was synchronous. For Urban, the fortifications of his military piazza at the Castle of the Holy Angel and of his religious piazza under Michelangelo's dome inside St. Peter's was intended to make the Vatican and Rome more powerful and beautiful" (7).

"More powerful and beautiful"—the expression echoes Urban himself. As is widely known, Urban obtained some of the bronze in question by stripping away the beams of the ancient *pronaos* in the Pantheon. After he did this, Urban erected a dedicatory inscription beside the main door of the Pantheon that is still in place. The inscription states that the building's metal had been transformed into columns inside St. Peter's near the apostle's tomb and into "instruments of public security" (*instrumenta publicae securitatis*) positioned at Hadrian's tomb, that is, the Castle of the Holy Angel. Urban's inscription captured in a single expression the military prowess he sought for his realm and the beauty he intended for the church. It was a beauty of biblical proportions, because the fluted columns that formed a most striking part of the baldachin were decidedly Solomonic.

Urban could have done none of this without his artists, Bernini and Borromini. In the construction of the baldachin, Bernini's contributions were modest (Bacchi 1998, 14–15). He was a sculptor, and the baldachin was one of his first architectural projects. Hence he relied on Borromini (Francesco Castelli), his architecturally astute assistant. They modeled the four columns of the baldachin on the twelve fluted columns that had been fixtures in the first St. Peter's and were again prominent in the design of the new basilica (Kirwin 1997, 135). Arguably the bronze columns of the baldachin embraced even more of the Solomonic legend, given their towering height, which paralleled the immensity of Yachin and Boaz.

5. Conclusion

The twin columns Yachin and Boaz were remarkable for their immensity and their ability to reflect the aesthetic and political sensibilities of Solomonic Israel. Aesthetically, Yachin and Boaz represented not merely

Left: Dedicatory inscription beside the main door of the Pantheon: "Pope Urban VIII turned the old remains of the bronze paneling into Vatican columns and war machines, so that [these] adornments, useless and nearly unknown to lore itself, would become the embellishments of the tomb of the apostles in the Vatican basilica [as well as] instruments of public safety in Hadrian's castle. In the year of our Lord 1632, the ninth of his pontificate." Translation courtesy of Walter Redmond.

Below: The Pantheon in Rome. Photograph courtesy of Martin Olsson.

beauty on a human plane but also the beauty of majesty, or that beauty associated with the deity, the God of Israel. In this case, the deity's presence in the temple set in motion a process of approval. First, the temple itself was by definition the symbol par excellence of the deity's support for a ruler. Second, the temple entrance, in various constructions, announced the deity's actual yet unseen presence in the recesses of the structure. Third, awe-inspiring columns at the entryway were thus the god's approbation by proxy of the local king. The syllogistic logic leads to the conclusion that the columns Yachin and Boaz lent legitimacy to the Davidic king and his aims.

Such legitimation was sought millennia later when two popes commissioned the finest artists of their day to incorporate Solomonic columns into the construction of the Sistine Chapel and St. Peter's Basilica. The later leaders associated themselves with Solomon's legacy in their efforts to establish their own rule over Christendom in the sixteenth and seventeenth centuries. In the pontificates of Leo X and Urban VIII, aesthetics and biblical tradition proved to be among the most powerful forces available to the vicar of Christ.

Works Cited

Bacchi, Andrea. 1998. *Bernini la scultura in San Pietro*. Milan: Motta.

Busink, Theodor A. 1970. *Der Tempel von Jerusalem*. Vol. 1 of *Salomo vis Herodes: Eine archäologische-historische Studie unter Berücksichtigung des westsemitischen Tempelbaus*. Leiden: Brill.

Cahn, Walter. 1976. Solomonic Elements in Romanesque Art. Pages 45–72 in *The Temple of Solomon: Archaeological Fact and Medieval Tradition in Christian, Islamic, and Jewish Art*. Edited by Joseph Gutmann. RelArts 3. Missoula, Mont: Scholars Press.

Eagleton, Terry. 1990. *Ideology of the Aesthetic*. Oxford: Blackwell.

Ferber, Stanley. 1976. The Temple of Solomon in Early Christian and Byzantine Art. Pages 21–43 in *The Temple of Solomon: Archaeological Fact and Medieval Tradition in Christian, Islamic, and Jewish Art*. Edited by Joseph Gutmann. RelArts 3. Missoula, Mont: Scholars Press.

Folda, Jaroslav. 1996. Crusader Art in the Twelfth Century: Reflections on Christian Multiculturalism in the Levant. Pages 90–91 in *Intercultural Contacts in the Medieval Mediterranean*. Edited by Benjamin Arbel. London: Cass.

Japhet, Sara. 1993. *I and II Chronicles: A Commentary*. OTL. Louisville: Westminster John Knox.

Jelf, Richard William., ed. 1848. *The Works of John Jewel, D.D., Bishop of Salisbury*. 8 vols. Oxford: Oxford University Press.

Kirwin, William Chandler. 1997. *Powers Matchless: The Pontificate of Urban VIII, the Baldachin, and Gian Lorenzo Bernini.* Hermeneutics of Arts 6. New York: Lang.

Kreitzer, Larry J. 2005. The Messianic Man of Peace as Temple Builder: Solomonic Imagery in Ephesians 2:13–22. Pages 484–512 in *Temple and Worship in Biblical Israel.* Edited by John Day. LHBOTS 422. London: T&T Clark.

Long, Burke O. 1984. *1 Kings with an Introduction to Historical Literature.* FOTL 9. Grand Rapids: Eerdmans.

Meyers, Carol L. 1983. Jachin and Boaz in Religious and Political Perspective. *CBQ* 45:167–78.

Monson, John. 2000. The New 'Ain Dara Temple: Closest Solomonic Parallel. *BAR* 26.3:20–35, 67.

Mulder, Martin J. 1998. *1 Kings.* 2 vols. Historical Commentary on the Old Testament. Leuven: Peeters.

Scott, R. B. Y. 1939. The Pillars Jachin and Boaz. *JBL* 58:143–49.

Shearman, John K. G. 1972. *Raphael's Cartoons in the Collection of Her Majesty the Queen, and the Tapestries for the Sistine Chapel.* London: Phaidon.

Tabor, James D., and Eugene V. Gallagher. 1995. *Why Waco? Cults and the Battle for Religious Freedom in America.* Berkeley: University of California Press.

Tanner, Marie. 2010. *Jerusalem on the Hill: Rome and the Vision of St. Peter's in the Renaissance.* London: Harvey Miller.

Wright, G. Ernest. 1941. Solomon's Temple Resurrected. *BA* 4:17–31.

Yeivin, Samuel. 1959. Jachin and Boaz. *PEQ* 91:6–22.

Beauty, Sorrow, and Glory in the Gospel of John

Jo-Ann A. Brant

> How beautiful, if Sorrow had not made
> Sorrow more beautiful than Beauty's self.
>
> John Keats, *Hyperion*

As soon as one begins to speak about the concept of beauty, one almost invariably finds oneself straying into personal aesthetic judgments about particular objects. We understand what beauty is through subjective experience gained through our senses. What I write below is influenced by what I habitually find most beautiful. I am drawn to Edvard Grieg's haunting composition that Solveig sings as Peer Gynt dies with his head in her lap. I found Joannie Rochette's performance in women's figure skating at the 2010 Winter Olympics transcendently beautiful, because her grief for her recently deceased mother was palpable. My tastes were formed early by the still form of Michelangelo's *Pietà*, the statue of Mary cradling the lifeless body of Christ in her lap. I am not alone in my judgment about the *Pietà*. Romain Rolland (1915, 127) writes, "Serene beauty arises above the sorrow." John D. Caputo (1993, 212) declares, "*Michelangelo* makes stone sigh with sorrow." While I do not find suffering in itself beautiful, I wonder at the ability of the artist to transform anguish into something sublime, something from which I do not retreat in fear. The author of the Gospel of John is one such artist. If one begins with the stance that John's theology contains within it aspects that may be described through the use of the current language of aesthetic theology, are we able to better understand the purpose of John's depiction of Jesus' incarnation and death? Moreover, can aspects of Johannine poetics, particularly in narratives dealing with grief, help inform a discussion of the relationship between sorrow and beauty? In my final analysis, I come to three observations: The unity of Jesus' and God's love shown on the cross draws from a concept of divine glory, of which beauty is an essential dimension. When death on the cross becomes beautiful, the followers of Christ come to see the presence of God within affliction. Finally, by rendering Jesus' death in beautiful prose, it becomes a memory to cherish and an event to commemorate.

Words such as *beauty, justice, goodness*, and *truth* are dangerous words in the context of academic writing that demands first the objectivity of an agreed-upon definition or standard and then empirically verifiable data. Modern Western philosophic tradition has relegated the discussion of beauty to epistemology. John Locke and Edmund Burke trace the complex idea of beauty back to the simple ideas of pleasure and pain, while in *The Critique of Judgment* Immanuel Kant focuses upon the cognitive act of judging something to be beautiful rather than trying to determine what beauty is. Kant acknowledges that beauty is universal insofar as we speak of beauty "as if" beauty were a property of the object being judged, but he severs beauty's relationship to the sublime and relegates objects of beauty to the status of decoration (§§23–29, 42). Given this Western propensity, a discussion of the beauty of John's treatment of sorrow is out of step with contemporary thought. It would, no doubt, be safest to write in Pythagorean terms and limit discussion to the symmetry and balance of Johannine prose. The availability of Greco-Roman rhetorical handbooks containing delineations of methods for writing sublime prose provides a standard against which to measure the beauty of Johannine composition. My discussion of John's Gospel, however, will not satisfy the demands of the positivist for empirical verification. The following discussion enters into dialogue with "pilgrims of the absolute" such as Simone Weil and Hans Urs von Balthasar. They recognize that we cannot point to the phenomenal world and say that this or that object is beautiful and expect all to agree. Nor can we come up with a definition of beauty that is distinct from the language that we use to describe other absolutes such as truth and goodness. Nevertheless, they dare to use the word *beauty* to describe the delight or pleasure of the senses when they are drawn toward something in such a way that all other sights, sounds, smells, or other sensations no longer intrude into one's consciousness. As Simone Weil (2000, 72) writes:

> [Beauty] feels only the part of the soul that gazes. While exciting desire, it makes clear that there is nothing in it to be desired, because the one thing we want is that it should not change. If one does not seek means

to evade the exquisite anguish it inflicts, then desire is gradually transformed into love; and one begins to acquire the faculty of pure and
disinterested attention.

Beauty's power is more mysterious than such things as might. It attracts
without our measuring the cost we must pay to be in its presence or our
determining how it will benefit us. By drawing upon the reflections of
various philosophers and theologians, I seek to illuminate the capacity of
art to render sorrow beautiful without reducing it to a calculus of pleasure
and pain.

1. John's Concept of Beauty as an Ontological Reality

Umberto Eco notes in his *History of Beauty* (2004, 9) that what we call
beautiful is often what we find to be good or virtuous. In order to keep this
discussion anchored in aesthetics and to provide some mooring within
Johannine thought, I begin with the relationship of beauty and glory
before proceeding to the discussion of the purpose of rendering sorrow
beautiful and the means by which this is accomplished in the Gospel of
John. John uses the Greek word δόξα when he refers to God's presence,
which is often translated as the English word *glory*. In classical Greek
usage, the noun δόξα is closely related to the verb forms of δοκέω (to think
or to be reputed) and δοξάζω (to suppose or magnify). A δόξα is a belief,
expectation, or opinion and is used in conjunction with the nouns κλέος
and τιμή to speak of one's social standing or the esteem or respect granted
one by others. In the Septuagint and other early Jewish Greek texts, δόξα
takes on another meaning when it is used to translate the Hebrew כבד, a
word that describes various aspects of the divine presence. Standing on
this side of the Copernican revolution and looking at God through the
lens of a post-Kantian epistemology, we have a tendency to consider the
elements of God's כבד that are associated with the phenomenal world that
we can see around us and events such as God's mighty displays of power.
But in ancient theology, כבד also described God's radiant, resplendent
being. Exodus 24:17 and 40:38 liken the appearance of God's glory to a
devouring fire enveloped by a cloud. Humanity in its sinful or fallen state
cannot bear to look directly upon God's full כבד (Exod 33:18; Isa 2:10, 19,
21). כבד is the aspect of God's presence that is perceptible to humanity,
particularly when referring to its dwelling within the tabernacle or the
temple in Jerusalem. The psalmist often uses the language of beauty to

describe this presence: "Out of Zion, the perfection of beauty, God shines forth" (Ps 50:2); "One thing I ask of the Lord … to live in the house of the Lord … to behold the beauty of the Lord" (Ps 27:4).[1] Walther Eichrodt (1961, 29–30) considers such texts that describe God's appearance naïve, but more recently scholars such as Richard Viladesau (1999, 26) and David Bentley Hart (2004, 17) contend that the aesthetic dimension of God's כבד is intrinsic to the joy with which human beings respond to God's presence (as in Ps 16:11). Might commands awe and penance, whereas beauty calls for rejoicing.

Many recent studies of the Gospel of John, in light of the importance of honor and shame as cultural forces, place emphasis upon the understanding of glory as a function of social status. Glory is dignity that is recognized. It is something given and, as such, is synonymous with honor, respect, reverence, and praise. In this view, humanity glorifies God by acknowledging God's supremacy. Jerome H. Neyrey works with this concept of glory throughout his commentary on the Gospel of John. For example, with reference to John 1:12 he writes:

> "Glory" means Jesus' worth, honor, and status. On the one hand, God bestows this glory on Jesus (17:5), which is the only honor that Jesus seeks (8:54). On the other hand, Jesus' signs manifest it to his disciples and require acknowledgment of it (2:11).… They "saw" this glory means that they acknowledge Jesus as Son and agent of God and were not scandalized by the shame of his cross. (Neyrey 2007, 45)

In this approach, the glory of Jesus' death is limited to his obedience to God or the performance of an act tied to the divine economy. Neyrey looks to socioanthropology for a solution to the oxymoron that God is glorified by the shame of the crucifixion by contending that the glory of God is brokered by the incarnation. Jesus has unique access to God and is the direct agent of God's benefaction. Jesus' bestowal of these gifts becomes proof or a "sign" of his credentials. When Jesus manifests his glory (2:11), he is making a claim to the honor due to God's agent, and his disciples complete the act by acknowledging this honor (45–46, 64).

While Neyrey has contributed greatly to our understanding of the role that honor and shame play in the Gospel of John, he does not address the emphasis upon Jesus' glory as a manifestation of divine presence and a

---

1. All biblical quotations are taken from the NRSV unless otherwise noted.

possible distinction between human and divine glory. In 2009, Alexander Tsutserov published a major study on glory, grace, and truth in the Gospel of John, in which he concluded that the connotations of glory found in the Septuagint account of the exodus story that entail God's visible appearance, as well as character, miraculous splendor, and honor, further inform the Gospel's references to glory (Tsutserov 218, 241). The Johannine Jesus frequently juxtaposes God's glory and the glory sought or gained through acknowledgment by people (5:41, 44; 7:18; 8:50). John uses forms of the verb θεάομαι (1:14, 32; 4:35; 11:45) and ὁράω (11:40; 12:41) to describe the act of looking at or perceiving God's glory. The narrator proclaims, "We have beheld [ἐθεασάμεθα] his glory, the glory as of an only offspring" (1:14). Jesus proclaims, "Whoever beholds [or looks at; θεωρῶν] me, beholds [θεωρεῖ] the one who sent me" (12:45; see also 14:9). John refers to a quality that both Jesus and God possess rather than the act of granting God a status. In order to exist, honor must be acknowledged (it is socially constructed), but divine glory is the aspect of God that is evident or perceptible to humanity. Therefore God's glory is not diminished by humanity's failure to perceive it.

The references to God and Jesus being glorified (13:32; 16:14; 21:19) and requests for the gift of glory in Jesus' final prayer (17:22, 24) present a challenge to this distinction between honor granted and divine glory. Jörg Frey (2008, 375–97) argues that John treats Jesus' glory from a retrospective perspective. Jesus is glorified at the hour of his crucifixion with δόξα that he did not possess before, but then John projects this δόξα back upon the earlier narrative. George B. Caird (1969, 270–71) attempts to resolve the problem by arguing that passive forms of the verb δοξάζω are intransitive and comparable to the use of a *niphal* form of verbs used to refer to God (e.g., Ezek 20:41). If we follow Caird's lead, lines such as "as yet there was no Spirit, because Jesus was not as yet glorified" should read, "because Jesus had not yet made manifest his glory" (7:39). Jesper Tang Nielsen (2010, 363) offers another way to untangle Johannine usage. Jesus' glory is equivalent to his identity. Jesus glorifies God by revealing God through doing God's work. After his glorification on the cross, his disciples can perceive his identity as God's Son. The possibility remains that John is not consistent in his usage and uses δόξα and related verb forms to refer to God's being as well as to the honor given to God by human beings. The challenge is to demonstrate that the tension ought not to be resolved in favor of the socioanthropological or ethical meanings of δόξα. It is also important to recognize that John works with a concept of δόξα that entails an aesthetic quality that is God's beauty in some instances.

In John, faith makes possible the perception of divine presence in Jesus. Hans Urs von Balthasar (1982, 247), in addressing the ontic relationship of beauty and revelation, argues that the grace of the Holy Spirit creates the faculty that can apprehend the form of God and "can relish it and fit its joy in it." Those who are attuned to the rhythm of God recognize God's self-expression in human acts and eventually in the incarnation (251). While one would be hard pressed to demonstrate that John envisions the bequest of such a gift in John 20:22 or at any earlier point in the Gospel, readers need something like von Balthasar's language of attunement (*Stimmung*) to account for the varying responses to Jesus' signs within the Johannine narratives. Just as sheep respond to the voice of the shepherd (10:3–4), the disciples are beckoned by Jesus' invitation to "come and see" (1:39), and Mary's joy is awakened by the sound of her name on Jesus' lips (20:16). The Samaritan woman shares in a desire for true worship; the blind man is prepared to see with Jesus' eyes rather than those of the Pharisees. Jesus is the light that shines in the darkness, a darkness that cannot overwhelm his light yet does not comprehend it (1:5). Without admitting the illumination he provides, the world cannot recognize or accept him (1:10–11). The glory of the Son is evident only to those who seek God's glory and who do not look at the world through the lens of worldly standards of honor (5:44).

2. FOUR DISTINCTIVE JOHANNINE THEMES

While no one text or tightly related set of passages prove the case that John works with the notion that God's glory refers in part to his beautiful presence, four themes distinct to the Johannine narrative point to the association of divine glory with beauty: the way that God and Jesus draw believers, the representation of glory as tangible, the temple motif, and the transformation of those who behold glory.

One of the more problematic claims in the Gospel of John is the notion that only those drawn (ἐλθεῖν) by the Father can come to Jesus and be raised up on the last day (6:44). Another is the universalism suggested by Jesus' claim that "I, when I am lifted up from the earth, will draw [ἑλκύσω] all people to myself" (12:32). In both instances, the difficulty arises from the treatment of drawing as synonymous with selecting, in which case God picks those who will believe and Jesus chooses all people. Augustine of Hippo understands the act of drawing to be not the exercise of God's will over the will of a human being but rather the effect of divine love. According to Augustine, divine love draws not by necessity but by "pleasure; not obligation, but delight" (*Tract. Ev. Jo.* 26.4, Gibb 1888).

In John, Jesus draws people to himself after they witness his καλός works (see John 10:32–33). Jesus describes himself as the καλός shepherd to whom the sheep are drawn by the sound of his voice (10:11, 14). There is a propensity to translate the word καλός with the English word "good" and, thereby, to emphasize the ethical or salvific nature of his deeds. But καλός signifies that something is admirable and, therefore, can point to either virtue or beauty. The temple police's claim that Jesus speaks like no other (7:46) may be either a reference to his ethical teachings, which John leaves out of his narrative, or a reference to the sublime quality of Jesus' oratory, which John includes. Jesus speaks beautifully. For example, throughout the arguments in John 5, Jesus uses figures of speech such as *epistrophe* (a series of clauses or lines ending with the same wording), alliteration, and *anaphora* (repetition of the same wording at the beginning of clauses or lines) that serve as much to please the audience of the Gospel and to present Jesus as an orator as to present his case. Jesus' language for himself—"I am the light of the world," "I am the living water," "I am the bread of life"—aligns him with things that delight the senses and satiate desire (4:13; 6:35). Those who consume the living water and bread of life participate in Jesus' nature (4:14; 6:56). John presents Jesus as a being who attracts and, in so doing, leads to a desire to abide in him.

Jesus' beauty becomes tangible in the signs of divine glory witnessed by those who believe. When Mary Magdalene peers into the empty tomb, at the spot in which Jesus' body had lain, she sees two angels. This is a vision suggestive of the ark, the visual manifestation of God's glory or presence (Exod 25:10–22). At the wedding in Cana (2:1–11), his glory is revealed not only in the power to change water into wine but also in the kind of wine he produces. It is good (καλόν) wine (2:10). We tend to focus upon beauty manifested to the senses of sight and sound, but beauty can also be perceived in scent, taste, and touch. On two occasions Jesus feeds people bread and small fish. Because of bread's association with manna and the Lord's Supper and Jesus' reference to the bread from heaven and bread of life (6:32–35), the significance of the fish in the feeding stories is often neglected. Jesus serves the five thousand a relish that makes the barley bread appetizing (6:11). The meal that he serves the disciples at the end of the Gospel is likewise bread savored with small grilled fish (21:9). When Martha expresses her fear that opening Lazarus' tomb will expose them to the stench of death, Jesus says, "Did I not tell you that if you believed, you would see the glory of God?" (11:40). The raising of Lazarus is followed by the story in which the fragrance of the nard with which Mary anoints Jesus' feet fills the house (12:3). Jesus' words transform her gesture of gratitude into the preparation of his dead body for burial. Jesus' corpse is enveloped in spices and one hundred pounds of myrrh (19:39–40), a kingly unguent with a long-lasting fragrance reminiscent of patchouli and valerian (see Ps 45:7–8 LXX; Groom 1997, 315).

The beauty of the temple is a prevalent theme in the Hebrew Bible and related Jewish literature.[2] As Walter Brueggemann demonstrates:

> The tabernacle tradition (Exod 25–31; 35–40) is preoccupied with beauty…. the tabernacle is made into a suitable and appropriate place of Yahweh's visible presence by the practice of a beauty commensurate with Yahweh's character…. Israel is summoned to worship in a holy place of unspeakable splendor (Pss 29:2, 96:9; 1 Chr 16:29; 2 Chr 20:21). The old, familiar translation of the recurring phrase in these texts is "the beauty of holiness." (1997, 426–27)

While John does not make explicit reference to the beauty of the temple, it seems probable that the notion of Jesus as an object of beauty would follow from John's representation of Jesus as the temple. The concept of beauty is implicit within the effect of Jesus' presence upon those who recognize him and trust in him. In the Gospel of John, the proper response to the revelation of God's glory is not awe or penitence but joy (3:29; 15:10–11; 16:20–24; 17:13). In the recognition scene in the garden, emphasis is placed upon the turn from grief to joy (20:11–16). Once the disciples recognize their risen Lord, their fear gives way to joy (20:20). Jesus repeatedly admonishes his followers to react to his crucifixion with complete joy rather than grief (15:11; 16:20–24; 17:13). In contrast, the witnesses to the resurrection in the Synoptic tradition feel a lingering fear.

John presents a picture of the restoration of human glory. Ezekiel describes the primal perfection of humanity in the lament for the king of Tyre as a state "full of wisdom and perfect in beauty" (Ezek 28:12). The tradition of Adam's pristine beauty also appears in the rabbinic tradition (b. B. Bat. 58a). When Jesus prays for his disciples, he states that he has given them the glory that he has received from the Father (17:22) and asks that

---

2. A number of major studies of the temple theme in the Gospel of John have appeared in recent years; for example, Coloe 2001; Kerr 2002; Um 2006.

his disciples see the glory that God gave him "before the foundation of the world" (17:24). To the early church fathers, this restoration of the *imago Dei* entails, among other things, partaking in divine beauty. Gregory of Nyssa describes being in the image of God as an "original comeliness … in the actually living face." The "beauty of goodness" is a reflection of the "blessed features" of that original beauty (*De beat.* 1; Graef 1954). Jesus' reference to the gift of glory calls for the unpacking of a tangle of allusions and complicated chronology. The Johannine Jesus habitually speaks of future events as past events. He seems to refer to a resurrection appearance during which he breathes the spirit upon his disciples (20:22). This act recalls God's act of breathing life into Adam (Gen 2:7). The Gospel's prologue also ties the gift of divine glory with the restoration of the *imago Dei*. The λόγος is an agent in the creation of all things (1:2), and the followers of Jesus are empowered to become children of God "who were born, not of blood or of the will of the flesh or of the will of man, but of God" (1:13). In his depiction of himself as the true vine in which the believing community abides, Jesus draws upon the tradition of the tree of life. First Enoch describes that tree: "This is a beautiful tree, beautiful to view, with leaves (so) handsome and blossoms (so) magnificent in appearance" (1 En. 24:5; Isaac 1983; see also 2 En. 8:225). Jesus' disciples make manifest God's glory by bearing abundant, everlasting fruit (15:8, 16). The image of the vine and the promise of abundant life in John 10:10 point to the re-creation of the abundance with which God blesses creation (Gen 1:22, 28). Brueggemann (1997, 339), among others, suggests that we treat God's pronouncement at the conclusion of creation as an aesthetic judgment about the beauty or loveliness of his work. The language that John chooses to describe restored humanity suggests that God's delight is an aesthetic as well as an ethical pleasure. In Johannine realized eschatology, God bestows the gift of eternal life upon believers so that the community of believers is the resurrected community. Those who believe are reborn of the Spirit (3:5) and no longer perish but have eternal life (3:16). Ancient Jewish writers consistently describe the resurrected body as something beautiful. Daniel 12:3 claims that the wise among those who are resurrected shall "shine as the brightness of the sky." In the account of the resurrection in 2 Baruch, the wicked will become uglier and the righteous more beautiful:

> The shape of those who now act wickedly will be made more evil and the glory of those who prove to be righteous … their splendor will be glorified by transformations, and the shape of their face will be changed into

the light of their beauty.... they will be like the angels and be equal to the stars. And they will be changed into any shape which they wished, from beauty to loveliness, and from light to the splendor of glory. (51:2–3, 10; Klijn 1983)

Paul states that God will change our vile bodies into his glorious body (Phil 3:21). John's references to eternal life are informed by traditional understandings of the resurrection of the body.

Taken individually, no one of these pieces of the Johannine tradition seems sufficient to warrant the conclusion that John's understanding of glory is informed by a concept of beauty. Taken together, the possibility seems reasonable. Moreover, if one posits that such a concept is at work, the place of these distinctive features of the Gospel of John within ancient Jewish and early Christian thought becomes clearer and the interrelationship of these features becomes more pronounced.

3. Beholding the Beauty of the Cross

Martin Luther and John Calvin struggled with the notion that the believer beholds God's glory and reduced this vision to a fleeting moment of inner consciousness. John's seeming emphasis on faith based upon hearing the word allowed them to grant visions of glory or to hear the voice of God only as a metaphoric role. As Hans Urs von Balthasar (1982, 57–58) notes, Luther wished to exclude the books that emphasized the aesthetic experience of God from the canon and relegated the *theologia gloria* to an eschatological age. Perhaps the modern dichotomy between spiritual or moral and material things leads us to disregard the aesthetic dimension of the restoration of glory as something delightful to which God is drawn and then to regard Jesus' manifestation of divine glory as something to which humanity is drawn. The true Johannine paradox is that this glory is manifest in Jesus' death, a death that his opponents intended to be inglorious, something so shameful and hideous that those who loved him would turn away in horror.

In the Gospel of John, God's glory is revealed not in his power to resurrect nor in the restoration of Jesus' exalted status after the humiliation of his crucifixion but in the crucifixion itself. Excellent wine and fragrant perfumes are established manifestations of divine glory; an instrument of execution is not. Deuteronomy 21:23 pronounces a corpse left hanging on a tree to be a curse in God's sight. Cicero writes, "the executioner, the veiling of heads, and the very word 'cross,' let them all be far removed from not only the bodies of Roman citizens but even from their thoughts, their eyes, and their ears" (*Rab. Perd.* 16; Tyrrell). The apostle Paul describes crucifixion as "a stumbling block to Jews and foolishness to Gentiles" (1 Cor 1:23). John treats Jesus' death as a manifestation of his love for others and his obedience to God, but he also makes Jesus' death an object of beauty. He anticipates the Christian iconographic tradition in which the crucifix becomes an object of art by rendering Jesus' passion into an object of beauty. The crucifixion and anticipation of Jesus' death are not simply poignant moments but occasions for the author of the Fourth Gospel to display the full force of his capacity to write sublime prose.

In several proleptic references to his death, Jesus uses two typological images from Hebrew scripture that are associated with beauty: Jacob's ladder and Moses' snake. With its footing in a place that Jacob names Bethel, God's house (Gen 28:12), the reference to the ladder (1:50–51) becomes part of the Johannine complex of temple texts. In Targum Pseudo-Jonathan to Gen 28:13–17 and Targum Onqelos to Gen 28:13–16, the ladder is a vision of the divine glory. In the rabbinic tradition, the angels ascend and descend upon Jacob. Therefore, the rabbis place emphasis upon Jacob's beauty. In a study of Jacob's ladder, Silviu Bunta (2006, 55–58) finds traces of a widespread tradition in which an engraving of Jacob's beautiful face adorns the heavenly throne of glory (Tg. Ps.-J. and Tg. Neof. on Gen 28:12; Gen. Rab. 82:2, Num. Rab. 4:1; Lam. Rab. 2:1). In John 3:14–15 Jesus compares himself to the bronze serpent that Moses raised on a pole and upon which the people gazed as a remedy to the lethal venom of a serpent's bite (Num 21:4–9). The serpent is not explicitly described as beautiful, but in the prophetic tradition the appearance of bronze clearly signifies beauty (see Ezek 40:1; Dan 2:32). Moreover, snake motifs grace many ancient Near Eastern and Greco-Roman artifacts. Philo of Alexandria contends that by looking at the bronze serpent one beholds "the beauty of temperance" and as a result is able "to behold God himself through the medium of the serpent" (*Legum allegoriae* 2.81; Yonge 1993).

Whereas the Synoptic tradition treats the crucifixion as the fulfillment of Isaiah's comment "there was no beauty in him to make us look at him, nor appearance that would attract us to him" (Isa 53:2–3) and trains the eye away from the cross itself, John continually draws his audience's eye to Jesus' body. Pilate commands, "Behold the man," pointing to Jesus' lacerated, bleeding body (19:5). John describes Jesus bearing his own cross (19:17). We see the soldiers disrobe Jesus before gambling for his garments

(19:23). We see Jesus drink from the vinegar-sopped sponge and then the final indignity to his body, a spear thrust into his side from which pours out his blood and water (19:34). These are all sights from which one would normally avert one's eyes.

True to the injunction of Greco-Roman rhetoricians, John matches his poetics to his subject (cf. *Rhet. Her.* 4.8). John uses elaborate constructions and sophisticated devices that pay homage to Jesus' divine status in his treatment of Jesus' suffering and its effect upon his followers who witness it. The action in the crucifixion is narrated with attention to focalization and the timing of information, balanced prose, repeated elements, and suspense. In the first view of Jesus upon the cross, John controls the mind's eye so that it moves back and forth before resting on Jesus: "They crucified him there and two others with him on this side and on that side then in the center Jesus"(19:18).[3] In the scene with Jesus' mother and the Beloved Disciple, the audience sees those who stand at the foot of the cross through Jesus' eyes. The vocabulary ties this passage into a broader framework of the Gospel's symbolically charged language: woman (see 2:4), behold (see 1:29, 36; 19:4), his own (see 1:11; 10:3; 13:1), and hour (see 2:4; 4:21, 23; 5:25, 28; 7:30; 8:20; 12:23, 27; 13:1; 16:21, 32; 17:1). The inverted symmetry of the lines γύναι, ἴδε ὁ υἱός σου (19:26), and ἴδε ἡ μήτηρ σου (19:26a), as well as the narrative introductions with their repetitive vocabulary, generates a rhythm rounded off by the final line ὁ μαθητὴς αὐτὴν εἰς τὰ ἴδια (19:26b). By taking the woman into his home, the Beloved Disciple fulfills Jesus' performative speech act. With great economy, the action is complete.

In his depiction of the offense against Jesus' corpse, John employs a strategy of suspense. He begins with the pattern of focalization used in 19:18: "So the soldiers came and shattered the legs of the first and the other crucified with him" (19:33a). The reader anticipates the violation of Jesus, but a suspension in the action brings short-lived relief: "But upon coming to Jesus, there is reprieve, when they saw he was already dead, they did not shatter his legs" (19:33). John then quickly adds, "but one of the soldiers with his lance pierced the side." The shock to the reader is quickly undercut by the surprise of the soldier: "and out came a flow of blood and water" (19:34). Rather than death and humiliation, Jesus' corpse signifies life (see

---

3. The translation of the verses from John 19 are my own. The NRSV translation tends to obscure the elements of suspense.

7:38) and quite possibly the temple from which the water of the spirit of life flows (Coloe 2001, 208).

John's literary art holds his audience's attention in a way that allows us to look at Jesus' affliction. The Gospels of Mark and Matthew capture the nature of Jesus' affliction when they show Jesus praying to God, imploring that he might be spared. They have Jesus utter the words from the cross, ἠλί ἠλί λιμὰ σαβαχθανί; "My God, my God, why have you forsaken me?" (Matt 27:46; Mark 15:34, uses ἐλωΐ). In her exploration of the nature of affliction, Simone Weil (1977, 442–44) writes, "[Those] struck down by affliction are at the foot of the Cross, almost at the greatest possible distance from God." John reveals that the gulf between suffering and divine presence is breached by Jesus' attunement to God's will (3:16–17; 12:27–28; von Balthasar 1982, 520). John's crucified Jesus is in control of his own fate even to the point of handing himself over to death with the words "It is finished" and by relinquishing his own spirit (19:30). Therefore, John allows his audience to recognize the presence of God even in death on a cross through this representation of Jesus' crucifixion.

4. THE RELATIONSHIP OF SORROW AND BEAUTY

However, a distinction must be drawn between the beauty of John's prose, in which he renders Jesus' death a beautiful thing, and the suffering that Jesus endured on the cross. John does not romanticize affliction. Jesus' suffering inspires the beauty of John's prose, but sorrow and suffering are not beautiful in and of themselves. When we witness real suffering or grief, we do not pause to rejoice in the beauty of the moment. Simone Weil (1977, 467) approaches the topic of the relationship of suffering and beauty from the point of view of their analogous relationship: "There are only two things piercing enough to penetrate our soul in this way [to the exclusion of all others]; they are affliction and beauty." The artist borrows from the capacity of the beauty of his or her art to pierce the soul in order to represent the piercing pain of affliction. In the week following the 2010 earthquake in Haiti, cruise ships continued to port in Haiti's secured luxury resorts. Owners did not want to deprive the country of the income generated by the tourism and used their ships to transport aid. Some passengers were not pleased. One responded on the *Cruise Critic*, an Internet forum, "I just can't see myself sunning on the beach, playing in the water, eating a barbecue, and enjoying a cocktail while [in Port-au-Prince] there are tens of thousands of dead people being piled up on the streets" (Booth 2010). The beauty sought by many tourists is the sort that obscures suffering. Simone Weil (1977, 457) writes, "Thought is constrained by an instinct of self-preservation to fly from the sight of affliction." Postmodern theorists use the word *simulacrum* to describe a sort of fabricated beauty that is devoid of goodness and truth, or worse, diverts attention from worldly suffering. In contrast, the aesthetic of the Johannine passion narrative entails an ethical response. Rome made use of crucifixion to arouse doubt in the followers of its victim and in the goodness, beauty, or meaning of the victim and his convictions. By transforming this ugly death into something beautiful in prose, John subverts Rome's intent. Death on the cross is not abandonment by the gods; it is not devoid of the beauty that draws the love of the gods. Just as Jesus gazes down from the cross upon the afflicted and lifts them up, God gazes down upon the cross and lifts up the crucified. As the study of films such as Leni Riefenstahl's *The Triumph of the Will* has taught us, art "can make evil appear beautiful and good" (Devereaux 1998, 251). But we also know that art can be a way to resist tyranny. John does not use art to obscure that which is evil but rather to expose it for what it is, in this case, folly. John shows that tyranny's attempt to belittle what is good by rendering it ugly through the humiliation and crucifixion of Jesus ultimately fails.

Spanish philosopher Miguel de Unamuno (2007) pursues a line of thought that takes him into the domain of consolatory rhetoric. He contends that hope is supreme beauty and supreme consolation. Suffering gives rise to hope. Love itself is a form of suffering, full of compassion and pity. When we love, we are conscious that the world we love is passing away, and this fills us with anguish. When we feel a sense of compassion, beauty arises as a form of "tragic consolation" (222). John's representation of affliction as something exquisite—something akin to a tragedy in which those who execute Jesus make an error—facilitates the commemoration of Jesus' death. It translates a horrifying death into a beautiful memory to which Jesus' followers are drawn and invited to relive through the reading and recollection of the Gospel's memorable language.

In its prologue, the audience of the Fourth Gospel is invited to affirm with the narrator that "we were spectators to his glory" (1:14a).[4] It is the presence of this glory in Jesus' person and actions, "the glory as of an only offspring of a father full of grace and truth" (1:14b), that the Gospel sub-

---

4. My own translation of καὶ ἐθεασάμεθα τὴν δόξαν αὐτοῦ.

stantiates through its representation of Jesus' words and deeds (20:31). John mediates the experience of this glory to his reader through the elegance of his poetics and through his use of biblical typologies that point to the beauty of Jesus' glory. As such, the beauty that meets the eye or ear of John's audience serves as an analogy to the ineffable beauty of divine glory. At the same time, John trains the senses of his audience to perceive divine presence in suffering and death by rendering their sight and the attendant sorrow as something beautiful to behold. In doing so, he provides his Christian audience with a memory to be savored, a memory to which they will return again and again in order to look upon Jesus' death as a manifestation of divine glory and, as a result, to rejoice in an event that, at its occurrence, was sorrowful for those who loved Jesus and whom Jesus loved. Therefore, we know beauty not by its adherence to a universally agreed upon measure but by its effects. Beauty causes the beholder to stand transfixed by a desire to dwell within its sphere and to hope that it will continue, unaltered by time. Beauty thereby obliterates the distance between heaven and earth and eternity and the present. Beauty cultivates a taste for all that is beautiful. It is the Gospel of John that inspires Augustine to write:

> He was beautiful in heaven, then, and beautiful on earth: beautiful in the womb, and beautiful in his parents' arms. He was beautiful in his miracles, but just as beautiful under the scourges; beautiful as he invited us to life but beautiful too in not shrinking from death, beautiful in laying down his life and beautiful in taking it again, beautiful on the cross, beautiful in the tomb, and beautiful in heaven. (*Enarrat. Ps.* 44, Boulding, 2000)

While the Gospel of John does not work this effect upon all readers, for those who recognize that Jesus is the Son of God, it opens up a vista from which one may contemplate a cosmology in which transcendent beauty is imminent even within affliction, and as a result, the Christian becomes drawn by the gravity of divine grace to suffering, poverty, illness, and death.

Works Cited

Balthasar, Hans Urs von. 1982. *Seeing the Form.* Vol. 1 of *The Glory of the Lord: A Theological Aesthetics.* Edited by Joseph Fessio and John Riches. Translated by Erasmo Leiva-Merikakis. Edinburgh: T&T Clark.

Booth, Robert. Cruise Ships Still Find a Haitian Berth. *The Guardian*. Online:http://www.guardian.co.uk/world/2010/jan/17/cruise-ships-haiti-earthquake.

Brueggemann, Walter. 1997. *Theology of the Old Testament: Testimony, Dispute, Advocacy*. Minneapolis: Fortress.

Bunta, Silviu. 2006. The Likeness of the Image: Adamic Motifs and Anthropoly [*sic*] in Rabbinic Traditions about Jacob's Image Enthroned in Heaven. *JSJ* 37:55–84.

Caird, George B. 1969. Glory of God in the Fourth Gospel: An Exercise in Biblical Semantics. *NTS* 15:270–71.

Caputo, John D. 1993. *Against Ethics: Contributions to a Poetic of Obligation with Constant Reference to Deconstruction*. Studies in Continental Thought. Bloomington: Indiana University Press.

Coloe, Mary L. 2001. *God Dwells with Us: Temple Symbolism in the Fourth Gospel*. Collegeville, Minn.: Liturgical Press.

Devereaux, Mary. 2001. Beauty and Evil: The Case of Leni Riefenstahl's Triumph of the Will. Pages 227–56 in *Aesthetics and Ethics: Essays at the Intersection*. Cambridge Studies in Philosophy and the Arts. Edited by Jerrold Levinson. Cambridge: Cambridge University Press.

Eco, Umberto. 2004. *History of Beauty*. Translated by Alastair McEwen. New York: Rizzoli International.

Eichrodt, Walther. 1961. *Theology of the Old Testament*. Translated by John A. Baker. London: SCM.

Frey, Jörg. 2008. "… dass sie meine Herrlichkeit schauen" (Joh 17.24): Zu Hintergrund, Sinn und Funktion der johanneischen Rede von der δόξα Jesu. *NTS* 54:375–97.

Groom, Nigel. 1997. *The New Perfume Handbook*. London: Blackie.

Hart, David Bentley. 2003. *The Beauty of the Infinite: The Aesthetics of Christian Truth*. Grand Rapids: Eerdmans.

Kerr, Alan R. 2002. *The Temple of Jesus' Body: The Temple Theme in the Gospel of John*. JSNTSup 220. London: Sheffield Academic Press.

Neyrey, Jerome H. 2007. *The Gospel of John*. New Cambridge Bible Commentary. Cambridge: Cambridge University Press.

Nielsen, Jesper Tang. 2010. The Narrative Structures of Glory and Glorification in the Fourth Gospel. *NTS* 56:343–66.

Rolland, Romain. 1915. *Michelangelo*. Translated by Frederick Street. New York: Duffield & Company.

Tsutserov, Alexander. 2009. *Glory, Grace, and Truth: Ratification of the Sinaitic Covenant according to the Gospel of John*. Eugene, Ore.: Pickwick.

Um, Stephen T. 2006. *The Theme of Temple Christology in John's Gospel*. Library of New Testament Studies 312. London: T&T Clark.

Unamuno, Miguel de. 2007. *Tragic Sense of Life*. Translated by J. E. Crawford Flitch. London: BiblioBazaar. First published in 1912 as *Del Sentimiento Trágico de la Vida*. Madrid: Renacimiento.

Viladesau, Richard. 1999. *Theological Aesthetics: God in Imagination, Beauty, and Art*. Oxford: Oxford University Press.

Weil, Simone. 1977. The Love of God and Affliction. Pages 439–68 in *The Simone Weil Reader*. Edited by George A. Panichas. New York: McKay.

———. 2000. Human Personality. Pages 47–78 in *Simone Weil: An Anthology*. Edited by Siân Miles. New York: Grove.

BEAUTY AND THE BIBLE:
SYNTHESIS AND LOOKING FORWARD

Peter Spitaler

In what ways did biblical authors perceive beauty? What made people and things beautiful to them? In what senses can one speak of a biblical concept of beauty? In what ways can beauty serve as a hermeneutical lens for reading biblical narratives? Answers to these questions are not as clear as I initially assumed. Rather, perceiving beauty in the Bible is like looking at light's spectral colors refracted and dispersed through a prism. One sees much more than if one looks at light passing through a simple spherical lens. Beauty refracts one's perspective on the biblical text—bends one's ideas about beauty itself.

This volume's essays focus on dynamic, reciprocal relationships between biblical narratives, beauty, the sublime, and the reader; they hint at the complex nature of research on these relationships. In some cases, beauty is the occasion of conflict and contradiction. This essay attempts to highlight synergetically some common themes and motifs in the various biblical narratives that my colleagues have treated and common hermeneutical insights among them. In particular, I will focus on the historical, social, and cultural boundedness of beauty constructs; subjectivity in the perception of beauty; and the relationships between the beautiful and the sublime. This essay will conclude with recommendations for further research on beauty, Bible, method, and hermeneutics.

1. BEAUTY THEN AND NOW

Both history and culture contextualize beauty, and culture influences the definition and perception of beauty. All the essays in this volume deal with the question of what it means that different societies organize their understanding of beauty differently. At least three interrelated insights can be gained from the discussion.

First, language matters. David Penchansky highlights a major difference between contemporary Western and ancient Near Eastern conceptions of beauty. In the former, one English word, beauty, functions in multiple domains: the human, the divine, and the natural. In the latter, different words must be used to express distinct categories of the beautiful. In addition, there are clusters of Hebrew words that share some aspects of the aesthetical but also include elements that are foreign to the English word *beauty*. In Penchansky's words, "If one takes these distinct Hebrew words and assumes that all of the words may reside in a larger category such as beauty or aesthetics, then one also lays down a heavy interpretive grid that forces many disparate concepts into the same anachronistic categorical space" (52). Jo-Ann Brant's essay demonstrates that the same applies to the Greek language system.

Second, depending on the scholar's research aims, Western concepts of beauty either limit or expand one's perspective on the beautiful in other historical and cultural settings. On the one hand, to actually see the beauty that biblical authors perceived requires the contemporary reader to know both Hebrew and Hellenistic conceptions of beauty, one's own contemporary conceptualization of beauty, and the distance between biblical and contemporary worldviews. Failing to do so may result in skewed, injudicious, or anachronistic analyses of texts and their contexts and shallow stereotyping of other peoples and their cultures. Penchansky mentions Gerhard von Rad's and Hans Urs von Balthasar's writings on biblical and theological aesthetics as examples; Brant cautions against Western preoccupation with objectivity, empirically verifiable data, and, in philosophic traditions, the relegation of discussions of beauty to epistemology.

On the other hand, to explore the relationships between beauty and the Bible by using the beautiful, or the sublime, as a hermeneutical tool for reading and examining one's experience of biblical narratives requires the contemporary reader to immerse consciously in an artfully designed narrative or rhetorical landscape. Antonio Portalatín and Jean-François Racine demonstrate that immersive approaches (reader-response) harness one's awareness of anachronisms and transform it into a methodological virtue. The reader interacts imaginatively with biblical narratives to perceive their beauty or sublimity; in the process of co-creating the beautiful or the sublime, the reader expands his or her own sense of it. Such approaches focus (on) the reader's experience and, Brant notes, encourage the reader to rise above the demands of "the objectivity of an agreed-upon definition or standard and then empirically verifiable data" (84). They permit participants in the search for beauty to realize that "we cannot point to the phenomenal world and say that this or that object is beautiful and expect all to agree" (84). Transcending purely positivist norms of empirical verification, especially those that stifle responses to beauty's attraction, the researcher finds beauty, or the sublime, in places the Western mind has forgotten they exist: in David's ruddiness and a lover's blackness (Penchansky); John's treatment of sorrow and death (Brant); Jeremiah's use of body imagery (Brummitt); or, in co-designing the scenery of a particular narrative setting (Portalatín); or experiencing the onslaught of impressions that overwhelm a character (Racine).

Third, in the Bible, "there is no single aesthetic, nor can there be" (Penchansky, 63). One's understanding of the sources of biblical beauty—the phenomenal world (human beauty) or ontological reality (divine beauty)—determines both one's perspective on and perception of it. This is so because "biblical writers incorporated into their texts different senses of beauty" (Bautch, 67). Correspondingly, Brant and Penchansky identify at least two different biblical (Hebrew) aesthetics—in Penchansky's words (52), a human ("ordinary physical beauty") and a divine ("beauty of majesty")—and note that exclusively anthropocentric descriptions of divine beauty, that is, with concepts borrowed from the physical, phenomenal world, miss the (Hebrew) perspective by a wide margin. The notion of "'beauty of holiness' … inhabits a different semantic world than the notions of human physical beauty" (Penchansky, 54). Richard Bautch expands on Brant's and Penchansky's findings, suggesting that the human-divine distinction is not absolute: "Yachin and Boaz standing in the sacred space of the temple are evidence of this fact" (70). That is, the Solomonic columns represent both physical and divine beauty. We might call this overlap of categories a third biblical (Hebrew) aesthetic.

A fourth biblical aesthetic appears in the Wisdom of Solomon. Influenced by Hellenistic thought, its author views beauty hierarchically, "where God's perfect beauty is on the top, and every other thing in the universe is beautiful or not, depending upon how much or how little they resemble or reflect God's beauty" (Penchansky, 54). Such understanding of God as a "source and pattern for all beauty" becomes the foundation for Western philosophical and theological traditions, which wrongly identified it as uniformly biblical. Still later, a fifth biblical aesthetic emerges in the Gospel of John. Its author merges the two distinct Hebrew aesthetics and produces one concept of beauty that is scalable across the human-divine plane. From this point forward, God's splendor and glory become increasingly enriched with anthropocentric concepts of beauty.

2. The Beauty That Biblical Writers Saw

Penchansky's and Brant's essays in particular show that biblical authors had little interest in systematic, structured reflection upon beauty. Nor did they theorize beauty. For them, beauty was less an abstract concept than an embedded construct.

Hebrew authors discussed in this volume used the word יפה to express "ordinary physical beauty" (Penchansky, 53) of both men and women. For them, the beauty of a person's physical appearance (eyes, face, hair, body, height, skin, flawlessness) was perceived or experienced; it was not a quality inherent in the person. Equally important, they saw beauty as a part of a complex web of relations, interwoven with patriarchy, hierarchy, royalty, power, favoritism, loyalty, gender, privilege, sexuality, and social status. That is, beauty emerged as the co-product of clearly delineated sociocultural patterns of reasoning and expectations. This tapestry of relations produced more or less predictable outcomes. A person perceived as beautiful had power (political, social, domestic); such power defined beauty. "The more beautiful the more powerful," Penchansky says, "and the ones who decide who and what is beautiful have the most power of all" (63). יפה never describes the beauty of God, not even metaphorically.

For God's glory and splendor, and that of the cult, the Hebrews used the words צבי and כבוד, which are rarely used to describe human physical beauty. Such "beauty of majesty" (Penchansky) was also contextualized (socially, culturally, religiously), appearing in genre-specific contexts (mostly Psalms) with references to other interconnected divine qualities (authority, honor, power, glory, strength, holiness, perfection, goodness, excellence). However, in contrast with ordinary physical beauty, which Hebrew authors perceived to be rooted in appearance, perception, and experience, the beauty of majesty was thought to be ontological. Brant observes that the word כבוד—splendor and radiance—not only conveyed God's visible appearance but also God's being and presence. כבוד is, Brant writes, "the aspect of God's presence that is perceptible to humanity, particularly when referring to its dwelling within the tabernacle or the temple in Jerusalem" (85).

New Testament authors (the works of Mark, Luke, John are this volume's primary focus) similarly saw beauty embedded in social constructs like honor, respect, and power. As is the case in the Hebrew Bible, Portalatín notes, "the cultural schema of authority ... influences the perception of beauty in the New Testament" (37). In addition, Brant observes, John also recognized stable correlations between beauty and capability (the deeds the Johannine Jesus accomplished as tangible signs of divine glory); beauty and goodness (what was καλός was also ἀγαθός); beauty and the senses (beauty manifested in sight, sound, scent, taste, and touch); and beauty and glory (God's δόξα as God's beauty). In contrast to the Hebrew language system, which uses different words for various glory categories, the Greek noun δόξα was used to express both human and divine glory. Thus, in John, we see a merging of δόξα concepts, creating a tension between honor bestowed (a social construct) and glorious being (an ontological category). According to Brant, John was able to use δόξα to refer to a quality of both Jesus and God, although by and large distinguished from honor granted through social interaction. Because John used δόξα to refer to God's glorious presence, δόξα is also in this Gospel "the aspect of God that is evident or perceptible to humanity. Therefore, God's glory is not diminished by humanity's failure to perceive it" (Brant, 87).

How does the contemporary reader know that words such as glory, honor, and majesty—"supporting concepts," as Patrick Sherry (cited in Penchansky, 52) calls them—were beauty words in the Hebrew and Greek language systems? Portalatín says that the motif of the manifestation of God's glory is central to the "repertoire of the aesthetics of biblical beauty" (40). However, on the level of the lexicon, glory and its supporting concepts have nothing to do with beauty (Penchansky), and individual biblical passages that have these words alone do not prove that a particular author "works with the notion that God's glory refers in part to [God's] beautiful presence" (Brant, 88). Penchansky and Brant directly address the lexical issues, Bautch and Portalatín indirectly. Combined, their answers both highlight the complexity of beauty research and provide some methodological guidelines.

First, the intricacy of biblical beauty defies basic word-study approaches. Links between beauty and its supporting concepts become apparent through analyses of themes and clusters of themes that point to the association of beauty with its related words. Brant and Penchansky conduct such analyses. In their expositions of beauty in the Bible, they piece together multilayered evidence which, taken individually, may not be "sufficient to warrant the conclusion that [an author's] understanding of glory is informed by a concept of beauty" (Brant, 92).

Second, Brant and Penchansky study attraction. In Penchansky's words, just as "the perception of beauty is an immediate experience," beauty itself is a "primal and immediate" drawing toward the object, an "energy that draws (what we might call) the beautiful object, and the one who perceives and experiences the beauty" (54–55). That is, the words that belong to beauty's support network describe qualities that make God attractive and draw people to God (Penchansky). In turn, studying these words and their interrelationships permits the investigator to describe the ways in which glory draws both God and people (Brant) and, thus, to discover and explicate biblical beauty's halo.

Third, architecture also is one of biblical beauty's supporting concepts. Whereas Brant and Penchansky consider physical manifestations of glory and might, in particular, the tangible, beautiful representations of glory in temple and cult, Bautch explicitly studies the relationships between aesthetics, theology, politics, and divine might, specifically, the expression of "divine might through a temple structure" (69). In his analysis, the primary supporting concept of biblical beauty is architecture that reflects the grandeur of political power. In other words, the Solomonic columns, Yachin and Boaz, exemplify the beauty of the divine and social power and might, and they serve an aesthetic purpose.

3. The Beauty That Contemporary Readers See

Brant and Penchansky use the concept of attraction to draw attention to the social, cultural, and theological embeddedness of beauty. Bautch also introduces attraction as a dimension of beauty when he argues that painters of the Renaissance period were drawn to Yachin and Boaz, because "the two pillars reflected aesthetic and political dimensions of the society that created them" (67). Attraction is also what Portalatín and Racine may have had in mind when they introduced reception or aesthetic theory (Portalatín) and reader-response theory (Racine) to explain the reader's interaction with the panoramic portrayal of biblical narratives.

Portalatín studies the reader-narrative relationship from the perspective of the beautiful (with insights drawn from aesthetic theory), Racine from the perspective of the sublime (with the support of various theories on the sublime). Their essays focus on subjectivity—the beautiful and the sublime demand the perspective of the viewer—thus reviving the Hebrew concept of perceived beauty. However, the beautiful or the sublime is more than the product of unrefined intuition or sensation. For Portalatín, beauty arises in the mind's eye of the *discerning* beholder. Likewise, for Racine, descriptions of experiences of the sublime are *guided*, not random. That is, the contemporary reader's impressions of the beautiful or the sublime may no longer be directed, or limited, by social constructs such as power and honor; they are structured by the mechanisms that the biblical authors "introduce[d] into the text to produce a creative reading" (Portalatín, 32) and by specific qualities of biblical narratives that prompt the experience of the sublime (Racine). Because attraction is visceral and precognitive (Penchansky), one's experience—at least in a scholarly setting—can be shaped by one's knowledge of these mechanisms and qualities. In other words, they can be analyzed and described, and beauty or the sublime can be experienced.

To describe the reader's participation in creating the beauty of a biblical narrative, Portalatín identifies and uses a set of predefined textual structures or mechanisms: social and historical elements known by the reader, poetic techniques, deviation, play between foreground and background, themes, creation of expectations, and frequent change of perspectives. In addition, Portalatín uses an element of aesthetic theory, pleasure ("beautiful images produced by the reader while reading cause pleasure," 34), to illustrate the experience of co-created beautiful narrative imagery. Bautch, Brant, and Racine also reference the concept of pleasure. Bautch and Racine incorporate it in their analyses; Brant ultimately considers pleasure to be reductionist for the purpose of her inquiry.

Similarly, Racine uses a set of criteria that guide the reader in re-creating the experiences of the characters in biblical narratives: novelty or difference, natural phenomena, association, fear and distance from fear, movement toward the "supersensible," and style. For Racine, the reader interacts with the narrative using these elements developed by various theorists of beauty and of the sublime (from Longinus to Immanuel Kant). Rather than working with one specific concept of the sublime, Racine uses the concept heuristically to describe what the contemporary reader may experience. Such descriptions of the sublime are scalable, and so is the experience of the reader.

Whether or not the beautiful or the sublime is innate in a particular narrative may not be self-evident. The sea, for example, may evoke serene beauty (Portalatín) or fear for one's life (Racine). Literary style may be indicative of the sublime (Longinus, in Racine) or arouse pleasure (Portalatín). Pleasure may be indicative of the beautiful (Portalatín) or the sublime (Racine). Fear may be the experience of characters in the narrative that leads the reader to experience the sublime (Racine), or fear may be part of a narrative's emotional landscape that leads the reader to pleasurably experience the beauty of a theophany (Portalatín). In any case, the approaches advocated by Portalatín and Racine combine the study of narratives as expressions of particular authors with a study of the perception of their works by the engaged reader who is critically self-aware of her or his role in co-creating the beautiful or the sublime. In this process of interrogating experience (Penchansky, 63), beauty reveals itself to the one who searches for it through distinctive interpretive lenses, "aesthetic in nature" (Racine, 21), and who together with the author of the biblical narrative perceives the beautiful/sublime in the very reading process itself.

Portalatín puts the reader in the role of a painter who completes the blueprint that is the original text and creates an "aesthetic object" (34). Pointing to the use of biblical scenes in the visual arts that reflect the imagination of the artist in interaction with the biblical narrative portrait, Portalatín suggests that the reader similarly is drawn to the text and fills in, adds, "engages the structures within the text, which by design lead the imagination and mind into the act of co-creating the fiction" (32–33), moving freely within, and at times perhaps beyond, the confines of the original: "Beauty as expressed by an artist or an author, and beauty as perceived by the reader or listener of the biblical text" (32). The fact that the relationships among aesthetics and imagination, invention, and creativity are not unique to the reader-narrative interaction strengthens Portalatín's metaphor. In his essay, Bautch analyzes the influence of narratives and art generated in the Near East on art produced in the West. Bautch concludes that Western art is not necessarily "based on historical accounts" (72); that is, beauty invites imagination but does not have to be historically accurate. For example, in artistic manifestations of Solomon's legacy, we see "a Solomonic ethos" projected upon European architecture and art. Artists sought "to fashion in their own realm expressions of beauty that were consistent with the sociopolitical realities of their day" (Bautch, 67). From a related but different perspective, Brant refers in like fashion to the "Christian iconographic tradition in which the crucifix becomes an object of art by rendering Jesus' passion into an object of beauty" (92). That is, unrepresentability is being transformed into representation through art (Brummitt, 26).

In summary, the beautiful encourages reinvention and reimagination of past perceptions of beauty and of experiences of fear and suffering that have been refined aesthetically through artistic expression.

4. FROM THE BEAUTIFUL TO THE SUBLIME

In addition to Racine, the concept of the sublime is of interest to Brant, Brummitt, and Penchansky. Each of these essays is rooted in diverse understandings of the sublime. They agree that the sublime is different from the beautiful in that the sublime is experienced through fear and distance, but disagree on the nature and extent of these differences.

Racine uses fear and distance to describe experiences of the sublime. He argues that fear or pain is experienced at close range (in his analysis of Luke 8:22–25 and 9:28–36, by characters in the text) and the sublime, including the experience of transcendence, from a distance (by the reader). Penchansky also refers to pain in the experience of beauty, "also loss and fear" (48), therewith acknowledging an experience that stands at the threshold between attraction and repulsion. Quoting Francis Landy, he argues that beauty "can only be experienced at a distance…. Yet it is also the focus of libidinal desire, for unification, for closure" (51). That is, there is an aesthetic tension between the longing for, and keeping one's distance from, the other. Penchansky does not label this experience the sublime but the beautiful. He ends his essay with the observation that "the experience of beauty creates a liminal moment—this moment contains great promise, great creativity, but also great danger. It threatens the boundaries of our identity" (64).

For Brant, the beautiful and the sublime are aspects of one continuum. Actually, Brant hints at a category of experience of the sublime that exists at the boundaries of the beautiful and the sublime. The attraction/repulsion opposition introduced by Penchansky may very well be at the core of this relationship. In her discussion of John's portrayal of suffering, for example, Brant wonders at "the true Johannine paradox," specifically, that "glory is manifest in Jesus' death, a death that his opponents intended to be inglorious, something so shameful and hideous that those who loved him would turn away in horror" (92). In other words, John is able "to transform anguish into something sublime, something from which I do not retreat in fear" (83). Portalatín also notes fear in the experience of the beautiful as being characteristic of the encounter between human beings and the divine. Glory, power, or might not only attracts or draws people to the beautiful; they also overwhelm them, drive them away (Penchansky, 48, 51). In the Hebrew Bible, "people who see the glory of God fear for their lives" (Penchansky, 53). This experience is embedded in biblical narratives, opening the door for Brummitt to investigate the role of the sublime in its relationship to "iconography of the sacred from Scripture" (24).

In his analysis of the relationship between aesthetics and the sublime in the book of Jeremiah, Brummitt, among others, works with a Kantian concept of the sublime that is contrasted with the beautiful. The sublime is that which disrupts poise and balance (qualities of the beautiful) "by dint of magnitude and power," that which is "endlessly outweighed by excessive meanings" (26). Thus, one may experience the sublime in the encounter with the sheer scale of an object (e.g., the ocean, a mountain) or in the encounter with "eternity in the decaying stumps of trees," an almond branch, or "the spill of a tilted pot" (26). Brummitt's essay highlights experiences of the sublime that signify cessation and death, expressed in Jeremiah in the "derealization" of the body, the prophet's body, as Brummitt relates it to the paintings of Bacon. Both focus on the scene of desertion at the foot of the cross. What ties Jeremiah and Bacon together is the body's brokenness as the locus of the sublime. Brummitt concludes that human suffering is not "something to be endured en route elsewhere" (29), which actually marginalizes the body. Rather, the sacred and transcendence are "a radical recognition of humanness with no escape route extended. Paradoxically, brokenness—not brokenness on the way to healing—is a locus of the presence of God" (29). God's presence in a body's brokenness means presence of the sacred in the sublime.

With the help of contemporary writing and art, Brummitt unearths the aesthetic dimension of Jeremiah's body imagery, concluding that the meaning of brokenness "approximates some notions of the sublime" (29). For Brant, in contrast, brokenness is another way of approaching the beautiful. Analyzing John's portrayal of sorrow, Brant notes that John "makes Jesus' death an object of beauty." John does not see beauty in suffering itself, nor in execution or abandonment by God. Rather, John responds to Jesus' suffering with "sublime prose" (83, 92). Through his literary art, he resists the tyranny of Rome, exposing it for the folly it is. Drawing the reader's attention to Jesus' ugly, tortured body John permits the reader to look at affliction and suffering and see divine presence manifest in Jesus' death on the cross. That is, affliction, suffering, an abused body are also in John not "something to be endured en route elsewhere" (Brummitt, 29) but the locus of God's presence. For Brant, in John's Gospel, "glory is revealed not in [God's] power to resurrect or in the restoration of Jesus' exalted status after the humiliation of his crucifixion, but in the crucifixion itself" (91). Brummitt would agree.

5. What Is Next for Beauty and the Bible?

The Bible, the beautiful, and the sublime relate to each other in intricate ways. The authors of this volume's essays show that it is quite difficult, and not always desirable, to split the beautiful or the sublime into clearly defined, distinctive representations or experiences. The outcome of their endeavors is perspectives on beauty and the sublime that are innovative and advantageous to advancing the study of biblical aesthetics. This volume is only the beginning of a very promising conversation; there is ample material presented that should stimulate further research. One may, for example, study the plurality of biblical aesthetics (I list five; there are probably more, with multiple nuances); use attraction, an aesthetic quality, as a lens for rereading individual passages or whole texts; explore the tension in Mark's Gospel between good news and fear as expression of the tension between attraction and repulsion; or read cosmic *apotheosis* and sky travel in the book of Revelation as expressions of the sublime. By way of conclusion, I would like to offer five additional, modest research suggestions that might advance, and possibly tie together, some of the various discussion threads in this volume.

Aesthetics of Ethics. Brant's and Penchansky's studies call attention to the necessity for a more contextually sensitive and accurate reading of καλός/יפה. New Testament texts, for example, have a significant number of occurrences of καλός (101 times) and καλῶς (37 times). However, readers of the New Revised Standard Version encounter only nine instances of the English words, beauty or beautiful, only one of which is a translation of καλός (Luke 21:5). The other instances are translations of the adjectives ὡραῖος (Matt 23:27; Acts 3:2, 10; Rom 10:15), ἀστεῖος (Acts 7:20; Heb 11:23), and πραΰς (1 Pet 3:4), and the noun εὐπρέπεια (Jas 1:11). The data are stunning. Brant is right; beauty is a "dangerous word" (84). Seemingly with ease scholars render ὡραῖος with the word beautiful, although the adjective does not have this meaning in classical or Hellenistic Greek. Simultaneously, they hesitate to resolve the lexical ambiguity of καλός in favor of an aesthetical rather than an ethical meaning or in favor of a reading that accentuates the aesthetical dimension of ethics. A possible research trajectory might start with the observation that New Testament authors ascribe a purpose to the beautiful and, because that which is beautiful is most often also useful and good, do not draw a line between the good and the beautiful. Whereas some things simply are beautiful—without purpose—in many instances, beauty is tangible and practical in so far as it is an essential quality of living: beauty evokes action. That is, beauty is not a private affair but benefits the public. The aesthetic quality of goodness shines through in most, if not all, instances of καλός.

Visual Christology. The essays of Bautch, Brant, Brummitt, Portalatín, and Racine encourage further research on biblical visual Christology, specifically the interaction of Christology with the arts, in at least two ways. First, biblical authors created the geographical, visual setting for Jesus' actions. Further research might highlight, for example, the nexus between "the sensorial image of the natural scenery" in the text and "the cultural schema of authority" (Portalatín, 37) beyond the text, or the biblical writer's social, cultural, and theological values. Second, the reader and the artist also aesthetically interact with biblical material and creatively enhance, even redesign, the narrative original. Research might focus on the interaction of visual art (both imaginary and actual) with, and its influence on, construals of biblical Christology.

Sensing the Beautiful and the Sublime. The essays in this volume make it obvious that in the Bible, beauty and the sublime encompass the totality of visual, auditory, kinesthetic, olfactory, and gustatory perception. The senses seem to function in more substantial ways than simply to provide support for concepts of beauty. Research might highlight the senses as constituent elements both of the beautiful or the sublime and of their perception. One might also study the relationship between a particular sense, or a combination of senses, and the intensity of one's experience of the beautiful or the sublime.

Production of Beauty. Bautch observes that the artist who created the columns Yachin and Boaz possessed skill (חכמה), intelligence (תבונה), and knowledge (דעת). These artisan attributes are identical with artisan attributes of the creator God, establishing a connection between the work of God and the work of the artist. "To make great columns … is to ally with the powers of God," Bautch concludes (76). New Testament authors also connect linguistically the production of beauty (ποιέω) by the faithful with the works and deeds of God and of Jesus (ποίημα, ἔργον). Further research might reveal the dynamic relationship between the performance of beautiful deeds by human beings and the beautiful deeds of the deity.

Body Beautiful. Brant's and Brummitt's discussion of embodied transcendence, or the body as locus of the beautiful or the sublime, might invite further study of body concepts in the Bible and body metaphors. For example, Paul's community-is-body metaphor calls for an investigation of the aesthetic quality of communal life and well being, especially because he also calls the community "temple of God." Beauty seems to be one aspect that unifies these metaphors. One might also further study the relationship between beauty and power. Since beauty is connected with the social constructs honor, respect, and power—and sacred architecture projects power—what are the political implications of embodying temple?

Having read these expositions on biblical beauty, I recognize my notions of beauty have been refracted and dispersed unexpectedly into multitudinous possible meanings. Sensing that I am experiencing an emerging edge in biblical hermeneutics, for the moment, I am content with beholding beauty's tangibility and elusiveness.

CONTRIBUTORS

Richard J. Bautch (Ph. D. Notre Dame) teaches biblical studies and Jewish literature at St. Edward's University in Austin, Texas, where he is a Professor in the School of Humanities. He is the author of *Developments in Genre between Post-exilic Penitential Prayers and the Psalms of Communal Lament* (Society of Biblical Literature, 2003) and *Glory and Power, Ritual and Relationship: The Sinai Covenant in the Postexilic Period* (T&T Clark, 2009).

Jo-Ann Brant received her Ph.D. in Religious Studies at McMaster University, Ontario, in 1991. She has been a Professor of Bible and Religion at Goshen College, Indiana, since 1993. She is the author of *Dialogue and Drama: Elements of Greek Tragedy in the Fourth Gospel* (Hendrickson, 2004) and *John: Paideia Commentaries on the New Testament* (Baker, 2011).

Mark Brummitt is Associate Professor of Old Testament at Colgate Rochester Crozer Divinity School, New York. He received his Ph.D. from the University of Glasgow, Scotland. He is a regular contributor to *Expository Times*. His research focuses on Jeremiah, Bible and culture, reading theory (structuralism, poststructuralism, gender theory, critical theory), and the literary reception of the Bible.

David Penchansky, a Professor at the University of St. Thomas, St. Paul, Minnesota, since 1989, specializes in wisdom literature and literary criticism. Since his Ph.D. from Vanderbilt University in 1988, where he majored in Hebrew Bible and minored in comparative literature, he has written about wisdom literature and theodicy. His most recent books are *Understanding Wisdom Literature: Conflict and Dissonance in the Hebrew Text* (Eerdmans, 2012) and *Twilight of the Gods: Polytheism in the Hebrew Bible* (Westminster John Knox, 2005).

Antonio Portalatín is Professor of Biblical Studies at the Catholic University of Puerto Rico. He earned his doctorate at the Pontifical Biblical Institute in Rome. At present he is completing a second degree in Comparative Literature at the University of Puerto Rico, and he is interested in interdisciplinary studies: reading the biblical text from the perspectives of aesthetics, literary theory, and theological hermeneutics.

Jean-François Racine is Associate Professor of New Testament at the Jesuit School of Theology of Santa Clara University, California. He received his Ph.D. from the University of St. Michael's College, Toronto. He is the author of *The Text of Matthew in the Writings of Basil of Caesarea* (Society of Biblical Literature, 2004) and the co-editor of *En marge du canon: Études sur les écrits apocryphes juifs et chrétiens* (Cerf, 2012).

Peter Spitaler is Associate Professor of Theology and Religious Studies at Villanova University, Villanova, Pennsylvania. He received his doctorate in New Testament studies from Ludwig Maximilian University of Munich, Germany, in 2003. His teaching and research focus on literary and social-science readings of New Testament literature, especially the Pauline and deutero-Pauline letters.

Index of Ancient Sources

NEW TESTAMENT

Index of Personal Names

CPSIA information can be obtained at www.ICGtesting.com
Printed in the USA
BVOW03s1236101113

335876BV00003B/3/P